D1125202

Weight Release
A Liberating Journey

The Powerful New Way to Release Weight Forever

FREEMAN MICHAELS

New York

Weight Release A Liberating Journey
The Powerful New Way to Release Weight Forever

ISBN 978-1-60037-691-7

Library of Congress Control Number: 2009934413

MORGAN · JAMES
THE ENTREPRENEURIAL PUBLISHER

Morgan James Publishing, LLC
1225 Franklin Ave., STE 325
Garden City, NY 11530-1693
Toll Free 800-485-4943
www.MorganJamesPublishing.com

Table of Contents

Please read the following, as I in no way
intend to mislead my reader.

True vs. Truth

In this book, I have used stories that contain truth but are not necessarily true. Some stories are fundamentally true but have intentionally been altered. I alter the stories for two reasons: one is to protect the anonymity of the individuals I am writing about; the second reason is artistic license. The characters in some of my stories are a composite of different people. The events are sometimes combinations of events rather than historically accurate portrayals. My aim was to capture the quality of truth as an illustration of human circumstances, rather than to be accurate in portraying past situations. There are some instances where it was important to retell the events accurately. In those cases, I may have sought approval for revealing the details from the people involved, or changed the names and circumstances just enough to protect their privacy.

Professional Care and Guidance

I am not a doctor. I am not a nutritionist or a psychotherapist. This book is intended to be "food for thought," or a new way of thinking about food. It is not intended to be a mandate for altering medications or nutrition plans that have been prescribed by a doctor or healthcare provider. If you are under the care of a licensed professional, I do not recommend you alter the treatment based on anything you read here, unless advised to do so by the licensed professional you are working with (or someone with equivalent qualifications). If you feel like you need professional care, I recommend that you seek it. This book should not be used as a substitute for medical or psychological treatment.

Acknowledgments

This book is much more than just the product of my own insights. The contributions of countless wonderful people who have profoundly influenced my life inhabit these pages. My gratitude is impossible to capture in words—but I will try:

To Tom Bunzel: I deeply thank you for your skill, your wisdom, and your friendship. The mark you made on this book is significant; I couldn't have done it without you.

To my family: My loving supportive wife Jasmine; my precious children, Josh, Antonio, and Isabella; and my dear caring parents, John and Alanna, you have given me more than I could ever measure. I am so grateful.

To my extended family, including my brother Jim, my grandparents, uncles, and cousins: The lessons we learned together were not always painless, but I love you from the bottom of my heart.

To my teachers, Mark Monroe, Jim Sniechowski, Joyce and Andre Patenaude, and Mary and Ron Hulnick: Your influence shaped this book as your wisdom shaped me.

To my two best friends, who have lifted me up with their love and encouraged me throughout the years, Tim O'Brien, and Chopper Bernet: You are tremendous blessings in my life.

To my men's group, Matt, Matt, Sam, Geoff, Fred, Sheldon, Adam, John and Robert: You sustained me with support throughout the process of writing this book; thank you.

Introduction

The Premise of this Book

Nothing is wrong. Where you are in your life is exactly where you are supposed to be. No part of your experience, past or present, has been a mistake. When you define your experience in negative terms, judgment* is clouding your perspective, which is a major roadblock to healing and releasing weight. This book is not about solving problems. The process I have developed, called Service to Self™, does not operate from a "wrong" or "right," "good" or "bad" viewpoint. From my perspective, you don't have a weight "problem," you have patterns of behavior that no longer serve you. The process, with information and exercises that follows this introduction, will demonstrate that much of what you have judged as good or bad, right or wrong, can be reframed and

---

* Judgment as condemnation versus analysis and/or discernment: Throughout this book, I refer to judgment, and I want to be clear what I am referring to, as the word can be used in quite different ways to mean very different things. When I say "judgment," I am referring to condemnation. I see judgment in this context as a negative pattern. Conversely, the word *judgment* can be used to describe a positive trait that involves analysis and discernment—this is often referred to as "using one's better judgment." For the purpose of this book, I am only speaking of judgment in the first context, as a condemnation. I am not speaking of the positive trait of analysis and discernment.

viewed as opportunities for growth and transformation. This new perspective will help cultivate a new relationship with your body and with food culminating in lasting weight release.

This is not a book about weight loss. I would not want to see you lose or give up anything. *This is a book about self-acceptance, self-love, and the journey to discover your authentic self.* This is a book about transformation that simply highlights one specific opportunity for transformation: weight. The aim is to reference weight but not focus on it. Focusing on weight makes weight the issue (and a problem)—but it isn't.

Following the exercises in this book should bring a general sense of fulfillment on a number of levels, and **weight release is just a natural by-product of the process**.

My Own Journey

Let me share a bit about how I came to discover the process I lay out in this book.

Not long ago, my life was filled with stress and I was filling my stomach with food. Over a three-year period, as my real estate development company faced serious financial challenges and potential bankruptcy, my weight ballooned. Bags of snacks and plates of food went down my throat without me tasting a thing. I stuffed and shoveled. Sleepless nights and depressed days sent me running for the cupboard. I found temporary relief from the excruciating discomfort in "comfort food." My weight became a profound outward manifestation of my inner struggle. Lifelong food issues were exacerbated by my situation.

I knew that I needed alternative ways to deal with my anxiety other than eating. It was time to take a good hard look at my relationship with food, my relationship with stress, and ultimately my relationship with myself.

The "self" that I needed to examine was defined largely from the "outside in." When I say "outside in," I mean the way I felt about myself was largely dependent on outer criteria, such as the balance of my bank account, rather than from inner criteria, a sense of wholeness and well-being. I measured my self-worth in terms of net worth, rather than examining my underlying sense of worthiness.

As my bank account shrank, my sense of self, as I had constructed it, began to fall apart as well. From a spiritual perspective, this was a true miracle and ultimately a tremendous blessing. The precarious state of my business had primed me for learning lessons that might not have been absorbed so efficiently and effectively had my circumstances been different.

Up until that point in my life, I had always manipulated psychological and spiritual principles to fit my views. I hadn't been truly willing to let go of my definitions of success and failure. My definitions of success and failure were largely based on what I was taught growing up by my culture, my society, and my family.

Whatever learning I acquired as an adult generally had to be adapted to my "programmed" beliefs. Despite having done a good deal of personal growth work, including earning a master's degree in spiritual psychology, I still understood success in terms of dollars and status. The personal growth work was conveniently adapted to make me feel more likely to achieve "outward" success. It gave me a sense that I had a spiritual advantage in my striving for financial achievement.

The crisis I faced forced me to give up my identity as a successful businessman to gain the wisdom that came from rebuilding my sense of self from the *"inside."* My inner work included sincerely examining my interpretations of success and failure. I began to re-interpret perceived failures as learning opportunities, both in the recent past and also in my childhood. I came to understand that it was my misinterpretations that caused so much of my suffering. And as I opened up, and compassionately embraced my experience, I began to feel incredibly successful—as a human being evolving in consciousness.

I came to understand that my wounds, those past events in my life that still held an emotional charge, were a collection of stories that involved a lot of misperceptions. Revisiting the past, with compassion for myself and all of the parties involved in my experiences, allowed me to embrace the humanity of my situation. I began to build a new sense of self-worth through self-acceptance and self-love.

The old adage "the truth will set you free" became incredibly valid for me. I learned that "truth," as I had previously comprehended it, had not, in fact, been the truth. I had misinterpreted many past events, as well as my present life circumstances, and I was internalizing shame and guilt, while projecting blame in a futile attempt to feel better about myself.

As the stories I had been telling myself, to defend the part of me that was ashamed and guilty, began to break down, I realized a deeper reality. I had the opportunity to *reframe* many of my interpretations. I began to see with incredible clarity.

I realized that I had been taking events *beyond my control* personally. I was feeling guilty for "mistakes." I felt responsible for other people's emotional experiences. I was ashamed to be in my financial predicament, and I was looking for people to blame. And of course, I was eating; historically when I got upset and began taking things personally, that had been my pattern. It took the breakdown of my identity as a successful businessman, to finally get me to look at my issues around food and around my weight.

What I Didn't Understand

Prior to my breakdown, or what I learned to *reframe* as a breakthrough, I had spent years in therapy, attended many personal growth workshops, and had been a part of several men's groups. But I had missed one crucial element as I explored my past experience in an effort to heal: *my judgment blocked my healing*. Even with trained professionals guiding me, I had misinterpreted the past. My judgment of myself and others left me caught in a cycle of shame, blame, and guilt.

During my years in therapy, tracking my wounds was painful. This experience left me feeling raw, but the kindness of the therapist—and the sense that I was learning something about how I had been wounded—seemed to suggest that I was healing. But I wasn't.

In uncovering my "wounds," I identified areas where I was particularly sensitive to other people's behavior. My kind and well-meaning therapist termed the behavior I was sensitive to as "toxic," as that was the identified effect we agreed that it had on me. The result was to create *boundaries*. Now, there is no problem with having healthy boundaries, but in this context, "boundaries" represented restrictions that I placed on myself and others in order to protect my wounded sense of self. I didn't know it then, but I was *negotiating* the world from my wounds rather than healing them.

I didn't recognize that my judgment (that people ought to be behaving in a particular way in order for me to feel safe or happy) was supporting my sense of myself as wounded. Furthermore, I determined that past events, and/or things that happened or were done to me, *should not* have occurred. I was judging everything that I was experiencing from a skewed perspective and I had an attachment to being a victim.

The Spiritual Psychology Perspective:
The spiritual psychology perspective is that wounds are healable, but in order to heal the wounds, a person must release the shame, blame, and guilt connected to them. Any attachment to right or wrong, guilt or innocence, or "should have" or "could have" feeds the perception of oneself as wounded. These are judgments, and inevitably judgment keeps the limiting interpretation of oneself as "wounded" locked in place. Most importantly, judgment is not loving, so it cannot be healing—*because healing is the process of applying love and compassion to the parts inside that hurt.**

---

*   This is a particular distinction I learned at the University of Santa Monica master's degree program in spiritual psychology.

Finally, judgment is not spiritual, because true spirituality involves acceptance of all that is without judgment or attachment. Yes, it may be important to track past events in order to heal, but there must be compassion for all of the "players" in the "human drama" (that is, spiritual perspective). Any and all judgments of oneself and others must be released through compassion and forgiveness (primarily self-forgiveness for misinterpretation). When the judgment is peeled away, only love and acceptance remain. In doing so, one can truly release the past, thereby creating a space for healing.

Compassion is an important part of healing, but compassion alone is not enough. Healing must also include activating a person's inner authority in order to understand what the person needs for self-fulfillment.

Compassion for one's humanity illuminates one's human needs without any shame, blame, or guilt. When the needs are embraced (rather than rejected and judged), people *tend to make different choices* to satisfy their needs in more healthy ways. Becoming more compassionate toward the part of themselves that holds the shame, blame, or guilt, they begin to release the weight of unresolved issues. When "checking in" replaces "checking out" and a few deep breaths replace a bag of Cheetos, weight gets *released*—not merely *lost*. By releasing judgment and making self-honoring choices, it is natural and effortless to release weight.

Men and Women

This book is written from a man's perspective (mine), but clearly the principles are applicable to both men and women. It is important to note that men and women have different programming. For me, as a man in this culture, my programming suggests that my value or worth is linked to my ability to make money. Women, in this culture, tend to associate success with their sex appeal and their ability to attract men. This is a broad generalization, and in modern times, there are many crossovers between male and female roles in society, along with myriad additional factors that affect a person's self-esteem. Though I speak from a male perspective, I hope that I have included enough of the stories of women clients and friends to make the concepts clear to both sexes.

I know the process well.

I spent many years trying to fix myself. I constantly lost and gained weight, but never really felt good about my body. My approach never worked because it was predicated on the assumption that something was wrong with me. The more I focused on the "problem," the bigger the problem seemed to get—and the bigger I got.

Most people change their diet because they don't like themselves, and they see their weight as an outward manifestation of their negative self image—and it is. They believe that by losing weight, they will change their negative self image—and they will, temporarily and superficially. But without true self-love and an ongoing practice of self-nurturing, no lasting shift in behavior will take place because their conditioned, underlying beliefs continue to promote negative perceptions.

Negative motivation is never a foundation for a positive self-image— and only a positive self-image will lead to lasting change. But positive thinking or affirmations alone aren't enough. The doorway to true inner healing involves compassion and self-acceptance. Only by embracing one's experience and releasing any residual shame, blame, or guilt can a person truly grow and affect lasting change. By reading this book, you will learn the principles and practices for success in this kind of transformational inner work.

By doing the exercises, you will begin to change your eating habits naturally, as you learn to love yourself. As you will experience, this is a different kind of learning, based on your inner experience and connection to your body—as opposed to simply feeding your intellect with information.

I recommend that you carefully read the "Getting Personal" segments; in these stories, you may recognize yourself. This should help you realize that what you're facing is not unusual and you are not alone.

In going through this process, subtle changes will become noticeable. Hopefully, you will begin to give yourself credit for things you hadn't realized, and reconnect with qualities you may have forgotten you ever possessed. You will also develop a more balanced and *less judgmental* view of yourself. You will find that instead of beating yourself up, you'll realize that in most instances you (and perhaps those you've blamed for your "problems" in the past) have only done the best they could.

Other things will change as well. You may see your life changing in positive and surprising ways, and all of these new *"yous"* will simply be a byproduct of you becoming more compassionate and more authentic.

Many people think being *authentic* is about expressing feelings. But I believe being authentic is about taking responsibility for your feelings. Feelings are only information. Feelings let you know if your needs are being met. When you feel "good," it is a strong indication that your needs are being met. When you feel "bad," it is a sure sign that your needs are not being met.

The Service to Self™ process is about becoming clearer about your needs. It is about taking full responsibility for finding constructive, healthy ways to meet your needs. When you are clearer about what you need, you can express your feelings in a more open and honest way. That is being authentic.

If you express your feelings without blaming anyone, people will be more open and compassionate toward you. If you start asking for what you want without making other people responsible for your happiness, people will be glad to support you. If you begin proclaiming who you are without needing other people's approval, the world around you will respond in surprising ways. Your life will blossom because you will satisfy your emotional needs in healthy and sustainable ways.

And food—whatever food has been for you—will change. Whether it has been your comforter, your protector, or your filler, it will find a whole new place in your life.

Now, stop and reflect on the following: If this prospect is exciting to you, keep on reading. If it terrifies you, then you may want to put the book down now; you may not be ready for this transformation yet, and that is fine.

Changing one's life can be daunting and you may want to simply have the book ready. Read little bits and keep it around, but don't commit to anything. This "warming up" to changing one's life is a normal part of the process.

The life you are presently leading involves various predictable components. There is comfort in the "known." Walking into the unknown (another way of describing change) is scary, and if you've decided to continue, give yourself some credit for courage. This spiritual "leap of faith" may change more than your own life—it may influence the lives of countless other people who grow with you.

1.
Why "Weight Release?"

Getting Personal: It Is Not about Losing Anything

A woman came to me looking for help. She told me that she had lost fifty-one pounds, but she seemed to be stuck at her present weight, and she felt that she needed to lose more. More specifically, she claimed that she "needed" to lose twenty more pounds. She wanted to know if I could help.

Initially, I told her two things. I told her that I couldn't help her to lose the twenty pounds that she thought she needed to lose. I also told her I was concerned about the fifty-one pounds she had lost. Her face went blank. She was clearly thrown. Obviously I hadn't told her what she wanted to hear.

My sense is that she would have dismissed me immediately after I said that I couldn't help her lose weight, but the concern I shared about the fifty-one pounds she had dropped kept her engaged. "Why are you concerned about the weight I have lost?" she asked with a touch of indignation.

I explained that I was concerned that if she lost the weight, then she would be looking to find it or replace it. "Oh no," she answered, "I am never going to be fat again." At that point I was even more concerned.

"Tell me about being fat; what part of that person that you were don't you like?" I asked her.

"I don't like how weak I was, I just didn't have the willpower to stop eating. Then one day I just woke up and decided that was it; I was going on a diet and I was never going to be fat again." She was motivated by her negative self-image, which, in my opinion, is not a good place to start.

It was clear to me that this woman held tremendous judgment against herself. I knew that if she were to remain the slimmer size she had become, she would need to have compassion for the part of her that had gotten so big. She must take the journey into the "self" she despised and judged as weak or inadequate.

I worked with this woman over the course of several months, and my sense is that she really did open up to what I was suggesting, but she struggled with giving up the notion that she "still needed to lose twenty pounds." I was able to help her reshape her view of food as sustenance and consider eating as a way of caring for herself. She created effective practices where exercise and healthy eating became viewed as a way to nurture herself. Periodically, I hear from her and I recognize in her words that she is still working on loving herself. I remind her that her relationship with herself is primary to staying healthy. Ultimately, I believe she "gets it," but this is not a quick fix. This is an ongoing process.

Getting Personal: No One Needs to Be "Fixed"

Another woman came to me. She weighed more than 300 pounds. She was very upset when we met. She didn't know she was upset and she tried to pretend like she was excited to meet me.

This was a woman whose sister had referred her to me—and she was suspicious. Her perception was that her sister was trying to "fix" her, and she was right to be concerned; that is exactly what her well-meaning sister was trying to do.

She was upset because I was going to "make" her lose weight. We talked for twenty minutes or more before the issue of weight came up. Frankly, I would rather it hadn't. Prior to the issue arising, she had seemed to enjoy the conversation, and it was nice getting to know her.

Finally she brought up the issue of her weight.

"So how are you going to get me to lose weight?" she asked.

"I am not," I answered.

There was a pause as she thought about my response to her question. "Then why am I here?" she asked.

"That is exactly where I want to start," I answered. I let her know that her sister's agenda was not my agenda. Her sister believed that there was something wrong with her, whereas I saw her as a wonderful person I was enjoying getting to know. My only motivation was to be of whatever service I could in helping her become the best, happiest, and most fulfilled person she could possibly be.

From that point forward, the conversation changed dramatically. Once she understood that I wasn't trying to fix her, she opened up. The truth is that she did want to release the weight but she was scared. So, from then on, we focused on what she wanted for her life. We examined her fears. We focused on her needs and observed her beliefs, but we very rarely discussed her weight. As we addressed her fears, wants, and needs directly, and focused on what she wanted in her life, her eating habits changed. As she healed, she made healthier choices and began to release weight.

"Weight Release" versus "Weight Loss"

Most "weight loss" books focus on overeating and lack of exercise; very few of them address the underlying cause of weight-related issues. These issues are a result of unhealthy patterns of behavior and a negative self-image. The Service to Self™ process, and this book, focus on reprogramming and healing old patterns of behavior to create a positive, lasting change, in self-image. "Weight "release" is a natural byproduct of this process.

This book approaches weight-related issues from a different perspective. As I've already mentioned, I don't want people to lose weight—frankly, I don't want anyone to *lose* anything. When a person loses something, they inevitably look to find it or replace it, right? The weight and/or the eating patterns have served a valuable purpose.

Let me use one common weight-related issue to illustrate my point. What if weight has been a source of protection? This can be very common when someone has been sexually abused. If a person has been hiding behind thirty, forty, or fifty pounds and suddenly they lose that protection, what are they going to do? Without addressing the fears, beliefs, and needs related to the protection, if they just *lose* the weight, they're going to need to *find* it again, or replace it with some other form of protection.

On the other hand, when a person *releases* weight because they have resolved issues and found healthy ways to meet their needs; it has the potential to be lasting. They must truly address the fears, unconscious beliefs, and the needs that perpetuate their unhealthy behaviors. They must find constructive ways to: 1) deal with their fear, 2) negotiate with their beliefs, and 3) meet their needs, before change will be lasting. They must consciously replace the old patterns with new habits (I call them *practices*).

2.
Your Relationship with Yourself

Getting Personal:
"Don't buy a scale, and if you have a scale, throw it out"
I went to visit a lifelong friend in the Pacific Northwest. I grew up with this friend and have known her all of my life. Part of knowing her for so long involves having seen her at various stages of her life. It was great to see her at this stage, with a husband, two kids, and a new house. But I had never seen her so heavy. Clearly, she was carrying extra weight.

Throughout her life, I had watched her weight go up and down. I knew enough about her history that I recognized a pattern linked to success and failure. When she felt successful, she tended to be thinner; when she didn't feel successful, she got heavier. Just based on that understanding, I knew something was happening in her life that was making her feel unsuccessful.

Sure enough, I came to find out that her business was failing. It turns out that the company she owns with her husband was behind on the sales required to be the licensed West Coast representatives for the parent company. She was doing all she could to try to improve sales, but nothing was working. She was taking it hard, and subsequently, she was being hard on herself—even eating things that caused an allergic reaction. I could tell she was beating herself up.

My wife and I were on a beautiful hike with my friend and her husband, along a ridge up behind their house, when she brought up her weight. I think she and I had been talking about the kids and school, when she suddenly turned to me and blurted out in a frustrated voice, "I'm going on a diet."

Without thinking, I exclaimed, "Don't do that!"

Suddenly there was silence. The conversation my wife was having with her husband abruptly halted and everyone just stared at me. I quickly recovered by saying, "If you want to change your eating habits, I support you, but don't go on a diet."

"Well, I do want to change my eating habits but I need to have a plan," she retorted.

"Yes," I agreed, "you need to have a plan."

"Should I buy a scale, to be able to see if my plan is working?" she asked.

"No, definitely don't buy a scale. You'll know if your plan is working by the way you feel," I suggested.

No one was talking other than the two of us; again my words had instigated an awkward silence. "Look," I said, "a scale is not a self-loving instrument; it only measures success and failure, which are judgments, and judgment is at the core of all weight-related issues." I spent some time during that hike talking about the principles I had learned, how self-love and self-acceptance were the keys to healing and releasing weight. I even followed up with some e-mails to promote my alternative way of looking at the perceived problem. I'm not sure how much of it she considered useful, but I felt I had to try.

I haven't heard from her in a while. My sense is that she is trying to fix things again. Her pattern is to push—to get motivated and try to stick with it until things change. I must admit that over the years, that seemed to have worked for her, but my sense is that the up-and-down nature of that type of approach is starting to wear on her. Getting a little older, it just seems to be more apparent that the pattern, (*losing weight and feeling good* versus *gaining weight and feeling bad*) isn't really working. I know how hard it is to break the success-and-failure belief structure.

This lifelong friend was one of the inspirations for writing this book. I hope she reads it and I hope it helps.

The Challenge to Change

The status quo is always threatened by change. This is true in groups, organizations, countries, and religions. But it is also true of individuals. Some part of us is comfortable in the discomfort we have created in our lives. There may be patterns we may think we want to change, but there is a significant part of us that is scared of the unknown.

Guts, determination, and a deep understanding that change is necessary can prevail. You *can* succeed in changing your life.

You need to know that there will be resistance, but if you are courageous and determined, you can step into a new life.

If you are reading this book, you are already on track. An *inner authority* has begun to let you know that you are capable of living life differently. The process begins with embracing the concept of "different."

It is the intention to change that becomes the seed of crystallizing a vision for the "new" you.

The old adage, "If you do what you have always done, you will get what you have always gotten," applies. To do something differently, you must first *identify* what part of your life is not presently working.

Your relationship with food is not working. The focus should be on the word *relationship*.

Relationship with Food

If the way you relate to food is not serving you, what is that relationship now, and most importantly, what could your relationship to food be in the future?

Food is sustenance and nourishment for your body, but it can also be poison. When you put food in your body that is not what your body needs for nourishment, you may be doing serious harm to your physical well-being. Food should not be a replacement for love, respect, or nurturing, but rather a fuel.

This is not a book about nutrition. For the most part, I won't be telling you what to eat or when to eat it. While there are countless books that can provide you with that type of information, I want to suggest you consult a more accurate authority on what your body needs: your inner authority.

Let me be clear: If you feel like you need nutritional guidelines, by all means pick up a book about the subject. My guess is that most people reading this book have enough relative knowledge to make good decisions about what to put in their bodies. In suggesting that you consult your inner authority, I am saying, "Listen to your body and use your intuition to guide you."

By moving into a dialogue with your body and observing your patterns, you can begin to link your relationship with food with emotional needs, and see how food has become part of a larger pattern of behavior. I call this process "checking in." I am mentioning the concept now, but I will go into more detail and provide a "checking-in" exercise later in the book.

At this point in the book, I simply want to suggest that your body knows better than any expert what it needs and what is doing it harm. I believe that "checking in" will provide you with a customized nutritional plan that is far better suited to you individually than any expert can provide. The most important part of weight release stems from your relationship with yourself.

Success and Failure
Weight issues are almost always about something deeper than simply eating too much or eating the wrong foods. Many

people who have been addressing weight from a purely physical perspective find that they are able to stay with a diet for a length of time, but ultimately the pounds come back. When they are thin, they feel as if they are happier for a short period (and they may be), but without addressing some underlying emotions, the unhealthy eating patterns almost always return.

The larger problem relates to the success-and-failure paradigm that they are caught in.

There is a measurement we subject ourselves to about success and failure—similar to the measurement that a scale literally quantifies for us each time we step on it. We have an image in our heads about what our lives "should" look like, which never allows us to just be where we are. We are constantly judging ourselves.

Your attachment to defining losing weight as "success" and gaining weight as "failure" exacerbates an unhealthy self-image. *Releasing* judgment means getting off the roller coaster ride; it involves getting to the underlying emotional issues. The process involves identifying the patterns of behavior and tracking the emotional connections to those patterns, then interrupting the patterns, addressing the emotions, and ultimately modifying the behaviors.

The entire process must involve self-acceptance and self-compassion to break the cycle of shame and guilt, to shift the paradigm from one of success and failure to one of healing and self-actualization. This will lead to a dramatic shift in your relationship with your body and with the world around you.

3.
Meeting Needs Versus Denying Them

Getting Personal: My Divorce

In my first marriage, I found myself in a deep depression. I had ridden a wave of "external success," and I was following a picture-perfect script. My bride was a model and actress. I was also an actor. We got engaged while I was playing the role of Drake Belson on *The Young and the Restless* soap opera. We had just bought an elegant condo in the hippest part of Los Angeles, right on the edge of West Hollywood and Beverly Hills, just off the Sunset Strip. We went to the "right" parties and wore the "right" clothes. But inside, I was having a very hard time. My "happily-ever-after" life was less than happy. A few months into our marriage, I was no longer working on *The Young and the Restless* and I couldn't land a new acting job. We soon discovered that we really couldn't afford our swank condo. We began fighting constantly.

I started to medicate with food—actually, I overate then starved myself. The emotional trauma I was feeling led me to traumatize my body by stuffing and starving myself.

To "fix" our finances (which I was programmed to believe was my responsibility as the man in the relationship), I turned to construction. I had been around construction all of my life and I felt comfortable fixing up and remodeling apartment buildings because my father and grandmother owned two buildings in San Francisco. I talked my dad into buying two properties in Los Angeles, and I put a crew of guys together to fix them up.

But my wife had married a soap opera star, not a construction worker. After one short year of marriage, we split up.

Going through the divorce humbled me, and I found an incredible outlet in a powerful men's support group. In my men's group, I began to relate to my needs. I recognized that the fantasy world I had created denied my needs—I didn't get to be "needy." I had been trying to play a role—the role of successful actor. I had an image, an imagined sense of what a "man" or a "movie star" should be, rather than what a human man should be. This was the first time that I focused on "taking care of myself." I often say that my divorce helped to make me "real."

A Commitment to Heal

The first step in addressing any issue involves a commitment to looking at the issue. A fundamental part of most food issues involves denial. Similar to those living with a drug or alcohol addiction, those who use food to try to meet emotional needs are generally unable to admit that they are stuck in a negative pattern that is unhealthy and self destructive.

> The unhealthy eating is not what people are in denial about. What they have been denying are their emotional needs.

Eating becomes an unconscious way to try to fill emotional needs. For example, if a person is anxious and uncomfortable, food may temporarily alleviate the discomfort.

Most people who are overweight or have food issues are aware, on some level, that they have unhealthy eating habits.

Human Needs

Emotions are linked to needs and wants.

Human beings need to feel safe. They need acceptance. They want people to like them.

The list of needs and wants goes on and on. Perhaps the first well-known psychologist to delineate these needs was Abraham Maslow, in his famous *Hierarchy of Needs*. Maslow's basic needs are as follows:

Physiological Needs

- These are biological. They consist of the need for oxygen, food, water, and a relatively constant body temperature. These needs relate only to the survival or death of a person as a living organism.

Safety Need

- When all physiological needs are satisfied and are no longer controlling thoughts and behaviors, Maslow stated that the need for security can become active. Generally, adults have little awareness of their security needs, except in times of emergency or periods of disorganization in the social structure (such as war or widespread rioting).

Children often display the more outward, recognizable signs of insecurity and the need to be safe.

Need for Love, Affection, and Belonging

- When biological and safety needs are satisfied, the next set of needs involves love, affection, and belonging. Maslow claimed that people look to meet these needs in order to overcome feelings of loneliness and alienation. This involves giving and receiving love and affection as well as the need for a sense of belonging.

Need for Esteem

- When the first three classes of needs are satisfied, the need for esteem becomes dominant. This involves both self-esteem and the esteem a person gets from others—also known as recognition. When these needs are frustrated, the person may feel inferior, weak, helpless, and/or worthless.

Need for Self-Actualization

- When all of the foregoing needs are satisfied, the need for self-actualization is activated. Maslow describes self-actualization as a person's need to be and do that which the person was "born to do." There seems to be an inherent need for certain people to make music, act, write, or paint. I call this creative self expression. Not meeting these needs can result in feelings of discomfort or disconnectedness.

Meeting Your Need

If you feel hungry or tired, it is fairly easy to identify the need to be filled. If you feel unsafe, unloved, unaccepted, or you lack self-esteem, it may be more challenging to put your finger on the need or needs that are not being met.

When there is an unmet need for self-actualization, the basis for the need (or expression that might fill the need) can be quite elusive. The Service to Self™ process is designed to assist you in meeting *all* of your needs, including your need for self-actualization, culminating in *becoming the "you" you were born to be.*

Food and Needs

For most people who struggle with weight, food has gone from filling a physiological need for sustenance to being a psychological means to fill an emotional void. The flaw is that food cannot actually fill an emotional need. It is only a temporary distraction that leaves the need unmet.

I believe that emotional needs must be filled from inside of oneself rather than outside of oneself. There must be an inner authority directing your life. No new job, new lover, or new object will have a lasting impact if there is no inner voice assessing the input and determining its real value. This process begins by first acknowledging, then tracking, unmet emotional needs. There can be a lot of resistance to this part of the process. It takes a lot of self-compassion to venture into the inner experience of one's unmet needs.

Tracking your behavior around food can provide important information about your needs. The following exercise is designed to help you recognize patterns of behavior around food and link that behavior to unmet needs.

Exercise: Auditing Needs and Self-care
Note: *Working with a Partner*

Many people find it is helpful to do work on a process such as this with a partner. In general, I recommend utilizing a partnership to promote growth and healing. It is important, however, to choose your partner wisely, and to establish very clear parameters for the relationship, as it relates to this process. It should not be either partner's job to try to fix or solve anything for the other person. This would be working against the process. The partner's role is simply to support the other. Please avoid the temptation to dispense advice to one another—as often projection can find its way into the dialogue. (I will speak more about projection later in the book). Your only job is to be a witness to the other person's process and offer encouragement whenever appropriate.

You may find additional support by visiting the Service to Self™ website and joining the Wintention community (it's free).

Asking for what you want, and having your needs met, is part of a larger strategy that I call "self-care"—valuing your own concerns and dealing with them effectively.

You will need a journal; it can be anything from a very nice leather-bound journal to a spiral notebook—try to get one with at least one hundred pages, as our exercises can go on for some time. (If you prefer, you can also type your journal on a computer.)

If you are working on a computer, it may be appropriate to e-mail the exercises or some part of the exercises to your partner. If you are working with a paper journal, you may want to simply e-mail a "progress report" about how the exercise went for you. If you are using

Wintention, posting your experience and using the forum to explore other people's experiences, can be very helpful and encouraging.

Another note about typing on the computer: In many exercises, you are tapping into your unconscious, so just write and resist the temptation to edit.

Start by drawing three columns (or on the computer, format three columns), as shown below. List the need in the far left column, how you presently attempt to meet the need goes in the middle column, and a possible alternative to meeting the need that might be more self-honoring in the third column.

Need:	How I presently attempt to get my need met:	Alternate, self-honoring, way of getting my need met:

As a general guide, here are some commonly articulated needs that you can use for the exercise, but personalize them for your own experience.

- I need attention.
- I need to have goals, something to look forward to.
- I need to feel like I am contributing to something.
- I need to be challenged.
- I need to express myself creatively.
- I need intimacy and to be touched.
- I need to feel a sense of control.
- I need some type of recognition.
- I need safety and security.

When your list is completed, write a brief summary of how you presently relate to your needs. Try to be compassionate with yourself. This part of the process is simply intended to activate your awareness of where you presently are and where you might want to go. Don't necessarily commit to anything yet; this exercise is simply intended to initiate a preliminary dialogue with your inner authority. You will have many opportunities throughout this book to expand your list and adjust your self-honoring strategies. Be sure to leave a few pages in your journal to add things to the list later, as the program progresses. Now share as much as you feel comfortable sharing with your partner(s). If you are using Wintention, share your experience by posting a comment in a forum or offer some thoughts within a specific group.

4.
Supporting Yourself: Intentions and Affirmations

Getting Personal: Bob "Saw Me"

Tears streamed down my face. My vision was obscured, my breathing erratic, and my body weak. I could not read what I had written. Mona had asked me to say a few words at Bob's funeral, but all I could do was sob. The impact of his death seemed out of proportion. He was not my father or even a relative.

As I stood there in front of dozens of people, most of whom I didn't know, I was paralyzed by my grief. I turned to my wife and handed her the paper, gesturing as best I could for her to read my words. "Do you want me to read it?" she asked. I nodded my head, as the tears flowed from my eyes. As she read them, my knees began to quiver. I held on to the seat in front of me, so as not to fall down. I sobbed. This was one of the greatest personal loses for me in my thirty-plus years on the planet. I felt like I was losing my biggest supporter, and I wasn't sure how to carry on in my life.

Bob was the father of one of my older brother's classmates in kindergarten. Bob and his wife Mona had met my parents while working on school functions. My parents really liked Bob and Mona, and they became lifelong friends of our family.

I was a younger sibling, and Bob and Mona only had the one daughter. So when we did family activities, the older kids often excluded me. Whether Bob felt sorry for me or whether he just liked me, I'm not entirely sure. But he often found something for us to do together that was just as much fun as what the older kids were doing. His warm smile and his gentle pat on my head made me feel special.

Throughout my life, Bob was an extraordinary supporter. I even lived with him and Mona when I moved to Southern California in my early twenties. I always felt great around him; I was *funny* and *bright*. I didn't feel especially funny or bright in most situations in my life, but around Bob, I just seemed to shine. If I had an idea, Bob encouraged me—often, he got excited too. He helped me clarify what I wanted and he consistently told me, "You can do it." He was my cheerleader—especially in the early days of my professional acting career in Los Angeles. I believe that his encouragement and thoughtful positive feedback had a good deal to do with some of my early success.

I say that Bob "saw me." He believed in me. He liked me—really, he loved me. How I felt in relationship with him became a point of reference for how I wanted to be in relationship with myself. I call the part in me that Bob "activated" my inner supporter.

Bob died a little more than ten years ago from cancer, but I can still see him in my mind's eye. I don't think he consciously knew what he was doing, but he taught me about being intentional.

The way he affirmed me supported my growth. I can still feel the kindness in his words. His encouragement touched a special part inside of me. I call on him often when I feel confused or need support.

Getting Intentional and Finding Support

You have completed your first exercise pertaining to needs. It may seem like I put the cart before the horse in having you do any work before you "set an intention." The fact is that the following intention process should make all future exercises much simpler and clearer. I had you do the needs exercise because I wanted you to do an exercise without utilizing intention in order to demonstrate the power intentions can have on your process.

What Does it Mean to "Set an Intention?"

The best analogy for describing the intention process is to think of life as a journey. When one sets out on a journey, one usually sets a course for a destination. This assumes that the person knows where they are going and they know where they want to end up. The challenge for most people is that they don't know where they are going and they are out of touch with their navigation system. Put simply, their navigation system is their inner authority, but they have lost touch with it. They are navigating their life by following directions given to them by outside sources.

We will go into detail about the outside sources affecting your life later in this book, but basically this includes the rules of society, the expectations of your family, the needs of others you feel responsible for, and quite a few other external forces that have been directing your life. All of that begins to shift when you focus your attention inward and begin to make conscious choices based on what will be best for you.

To set an intention and begin this journey, we will start very simply with what we know that you want: to heal and to release weight. The intention process is used to direct your life on a course where your wants and needs get fulfilled.

Setting an Intention to Heal and Release Weight

An intention, rooted in an inner authority, can be immensely powerful. But in order to embark upon the journey inward, a person must be willing to *accept* what they discover. In the preceding exercise, you may well have become aware of needs that you had ignored, forgotten, put aside, or suppressed.

When one has been denying something, there is a fundamental judgment standing in the way. The person is actually judging their needs – there is often a deeply held belief that the needs are unacceptable (e.g. it is not okay to need help, it is not okay to want attention, etc.). Lifting the judgment can be difficult, because often the judgment has been formed over many years. But self-compassion can only emerge when judgments are released.

This process *supports* you in examining judgments from a new perspective. *Setting an intention to heal* is a great first step in "working your process."

Saying or writing an intention to *support* oneself may seem corny, but it has been scientifically proven to be effective. Lynne McTaggart, in her book *The Intention Experiment,* outlines a series of scientific studies on the impact a sustained thought can have on effecting change. The evidence is compelling. *(See appendix to reference her work.)*

Exercise: Your First Intention

I am going to keep this very simple by offering you an intention to begin the process. At any point, you may adjust or adapt this intention to match your authentic desire to heal.

"My intention is to do whatever it takes to heal and release weight."

Please print or write the intention twice on two slips of paper; use each as a bookmark for this book and your journal. Whenever you pick up the book or use your journal, I would like you to read the intention several times—once you have it memorized, it may help to close your eyes and say it out loud.

Affirmations Support a Positive Point of View

Now that you have set your first intention, it is important to establish "affirmations." An affirmation is positive statement repeated over a period of time to instill inner strength and reinforce a positive perspective. All of the work we do in the Service to Self™ process is framed in positive terms. The premise is simply that we choose to focus on what we want, rather than what we don't want. As mentioned in the introduction, one cannot arrive at a positive outcome by focusing on the negative. I often say, "In order to find fulfillment, you must be leading with your strengths."

> When you focus on what you don't want, you tend to attract more of what you don't want into your life.

There is a subtle difference between an *intention* and an *affirmation*. Your intention, for example, may be something such as, "My intention is to totally accept myself, and to release my judgment of myself as fat." This type of intention might be very important in later exercises in this book, when we ask you to *reframe* a negative belief by applying compassion and understanding to your situation. This type of intention can be supported and greatly strengthened through the use of an *affirmation* such as the one we will be working with below.

For our purposes, we are going to use the simple sentence:

"I am a valuable human being worthy of love and acceptance."

Affirmations Combined with Intentions

Affirmations can be combined with intentions to create a positive statement that propels a person forward in life. As you work on creating more personal intentions that have a particular resonance with your inner authority, you may want to infuse affirmation into your intentions.

Begin with a general intention that *recognizes* the positive spirit you bring to the work and supports the general qualities you want in your life.

"I *acknowledge* myself and the choices I have made, and now make the choice to grow."

"I *reframe* my negative self-image and know that I am worthy of love and acceptance."

"I *celebrate* life as my teacher and I am open to learning the lessons that will make me a wiser person."

"I *recognize* my determination in making positive changes and the progress I have already made."

When you empower your intention with positive statements, your future begins to become a potentiality it was not before you reframed it with intent. Things turn from *wishes* or *fantasies* into clear visions of your future through positive intentions.

Exercise: Bolster Intention through Affirmation

For thousands of years, Eastern religions have used a spiritual practice called a "mantra" to bring about positive transformation. It is wonderful that science is starting to prove spiritual principles. Brain scans are able to track chemical reactions in the brain when a person focuses on something positive and uplifting. In fact, drug companies are making billions of dollars by synthetically reproducing the chemical effect of positive thinking. I am not a scientist, so I won't attempt to explain the precise chemicals or how the receptors and neurotransmitters actually work, but I have included some wonderful references in the appendix of this book, if you feel like exploring this fascinating field. What I do understand well enough to discuss here is that my positive intention influences my experience. There seems to be a relationship between positive results and a clear positive intention. As you continue to read this book and do these exercises, you will begin to discover it for yourself—my sense is that you may experience some amazing transformations.

Think about it: If someone repeatedly told you that you were not good at some task, skill, or activity as a child, the chances are strong that you would avoid it—and if you did attempt that certain task, skill, or activity, chances are you would not have the confidence to succeed.

That is called *negative reinforcement,* and anyone who has experienced it can attest to its power. Well, the same is true of positive reinforcement. Affirmations repeated and supported have the power to create positive outcomes. Using the Service to Self™ process, you are going to change your experience by introducing positive thought.

This is just the first of many affirmations, but the habit of focusing your mind on something positive is important because it becomes part of a pattern. Presently, there is probably a pattern of negative self-talk, stemming from messages you may have received such as "you are not good enough" or "you are not smart enough," etc. In this exercise, we are introducing a conscious pattern of positive self-talk. Later, we will actively pursue the negative self-talk and work to dispel its power.

• **Post it:** Please print or write out the affirmation, "I am a valuable human being worthy of love and acceptance" and post it in a place where you will see it daily—potentially several times a day. If your living environment involves shared space and you don't feel comfortable with others seeing your affirmation, consider putting it inside of a closet that you enter to get clothes (this way, you will see it in the morning when you get dressed).

I have a pull chain in my closet that has an affirmation attached to it. Every morning when I open my closet to find clothes, I pull the chain and there is my affirmation (I laminated it so that it could last). I have come to *acknowledge* the positive effect of reminding myself to love myself.

I have affirmations and intentions posted on my mirror in the bathroom and above my computer in my office. I have a friend who made a decorative collage with an affirmation then took a picture of it and he has it as a screen saver on his computer.

• **Say it:** Be sure to repeat your affirmation(s) several times a day. It often helps to close your eyes and make it a mantra, really allowing it to penetrate into your unconscious. If it feels silly, *release* the judgment, by simply saying, "I forgive myself for judging myself," and then transition right into the affirmation.

• **Remember it:** Remember, it is your relationship with yourself that is truly the issue. Overeating is simply the result of your negative relationship with yourself.

Negativity comes from a basic disconnection from a *truth about yourself*—that without doing anything, purely by being alive, you are worthy of love and acceptance by others and yourself. (In spiritual or religious traditions, this is often expressed as "God's love"—you are a child of God).

The source of this truth (from which you have become disconnected) lies in your feelings; we will discuss this at length in future chapters. Defense mechanisms learned in childhood are still protecting you. Perhaps teenage notions of *winners* and *losers* are still motivating you. Think about how similar the winner/ loser dichotomy is to success/failure, and how it's measured— and on whose scale.

In general, you are still aligned with interpretations of reality that you may be ready to grow out of. The next chapter will deal with interpretations and move you into a more affirming perception of the past.

Let me suggest again that if you think the part of your life that needs to change relates simply to eating too much or not exercising, you're wrong. Your weight is a symptom of a much deeper issue.

> Science is starting to confirm what spiritual psychology holds as a definite truth - holding a focused thought influences the potentiality of an intended outcome occurring.

5.

Resistance

Getting Personal: "Getting to the Gold"

"I don't want to," I proclaimed.

"I know you don't want to, but it may do you some good," the gentle voice answered back.

"Why?" I pouted, as if I were five again.

"Because I sense that there is a lot in there that needs to come out," he responded.

"I know. Okay I will, but you know I don't want to," I said.

"I'm well aware of that," he replied, even kinder and gentler than before.

He was so kind, so encouraging. I didn't know this man, but I trusted him. Tears began to stream down my face. Then from deep in my belly came a profound primal scream. My body began to quiver and shake. From behind me, another man wrapped his arms around me as I released emotions—anger, fear, sadness.

Over a three-day period, I negotiated with my resistance as I allowed myself to feel feelings that had been buried for decades.

I had signed up for the Men's Weekend with my nineteen-year-old stepson, to instill a few valuable lessons. I felt like I had already "figured myself out"; I simply believed that I was doing it for him. What I discovered about myself—baring my soul to total strangers at a Southern California retreat for men—was where my "gold" was buried.

The "gold" is a sacred gift that lies hidden in every man's (or woman's) psyche. My gold, I discovered, lay right on the other side of my resistance.

When Resistance Comes Up

Some of you may have had a very hard time working on the intentions and affirmations. Congratulations—you have met some resistance. When resistance comes up, I like to say "school is in session."

The first thing you should know is that resistance is normal. Honestly, I thought the affirmation and intention stuff was nuts when I was first introduced to it. I was so resistant to recognizing and acknowledging myself. I also had huge resistance to going for what I wanted in my life. Moving into a dialogue with my resistance, I discovered that I did not feel deserving, and that I did not feel capable of achieving my dreams. I uncovered layers of negative messages that I had bought into.

My life has changed so profoundly since I began the process of positive self-talk (affirmations) and making conscious choices (intention) that I can hardly believe it.

The truth is that there is valuable information in resistance. Part of your relationship with yourself must include having a relationship with your resistance. You don't want to be in denial. Let your resistance give you feedback about your programming.

In doing the following exercise, you will explore your resistance and allow it to be your teacher. Again, you don't need to do anything with the information you uncover at this point in the Service to Self™ program—just *observe* it. We will be working with the messages you find as you explore your resistance later in the book.

Ongoing Exercise: Give Resistance a Voice
You will need your journal. This exercise may be used often during the course of the Service to Self™ process. In other words, when you meet with resistance, you can use this exercise as a tool to overcome it and learn more about yourself. At any point in this program, you can take a few pages (even in the middle of some other process) to have a dialogue with your resistance.

Each of us has a naysayer inside of us ready to jump on us, whenever we open ourselves up to change. Introspection, focused on uncovering judgment, will in all likelihood meet with resistance. The best way I know to move through the resistance is to "give it a voice."

This is a type of stream-of-consciousness writing* starting with the premise, "I am experiencing resistance, and my intention is to give it a voice." Then, whatever comes up, write it down. Examples might include, "this feels corny," "I feel foolish," and so on. You will know when to stop when you start getting to feelings such as "I feel scared," or "I feel overwhelmed." When you arrive at those feelings, you have uncovered the underlying vulnerability that your judgments have been trying to protect you from. We will work with those judgments in due course. For right now, just get in touch with the vulnerability and observe it. You are slowly moving into the depth of your experience, and other tools that you will be learning later in this book will be important in shifting your energy and promoting your healing.

Note about Breaking Down Judgment
Giving resistance a voice is about breaking down your judgments. This is a little bit like developing a new muscle; initially, it is hard, painful, and often leaves you sore. During the course of your work with the Service to Self™ process, you will become more and more adept at: recognizing resistance, identifying the judgments, surrendering to what is underneath the judgment, and then forgiving yourself for judging yourself.

---

* Stream-of-consciousness writing can be an incredible tool to unlock unconscious beliefs. It is important to allow your mind to wander into the rarely accessed messages that may be "running the show." Just try to let the words flow; don't edit yourself. If frustration or confusion comes up, write down, "I am feeling frustrated" or "I am so confused." Just keep writing and let yourself explore. You will get better and better at this type of processing as the program continues.

The feelings underneath the judgment are what we refer to as the "truth." Just note that throughout the process, when you work with self-forgiveness to release judgments, you can follow each self-forgiveness with the prompt "and the truth is…" Whatever the truth is, embrace it—it will set you free. Here is an example of this dialogue: "I forgive myself for judging myself as mean. The truth is that I was scared and hurt."

Exploring the truth may make you feel incredibly vulnerable. It is important to embrace your vulnerability. This will help ground you in a deeper understanding of your humanity, which is healing. Remember, judgments are defensive—we take them on to try to protect ourselves.

6.
Recognizing Misinterpretations

Getting Personal: I Was a Chubby Kid

In the introduction, I said that I have had lifelong issues with food. For many years, I reported that I was chubby as a child. What I understand now is that the story about my chubbiness represented a kind of shame I had about my childhood in general. I formed a belief that I lacked self-control around food, which I would report caused a weight problem.

Surprisingly, however, I came to learn that I didn't have a weight problem; I only *thought* I did.

In the fifth grade, there was a group of kids who called me "Fat Ass Freeman." This particular teasing really upset me, so of course, they kept doing it. My memory up until recently was that I was overweight during that period. The mental image in my head, however, did not match reality.

Recently I had the opportunity to look through a box of pictures my parents had taken during my childhood. My wife was with me as I thumbed through the snapshots, and she was the one to notice it. "You weren't really overweight as a kid," she remarked.

"Actually," she went on, "you look like you were sort of the perfect size."

To my astonishment, she was right. It was as if focus suddenly came to my eyes and I saw the truth. I *recognized* that I was not at all fat. Moreover, I was very nicely built. I was not skinny, but I was by no means as chubby as I had remembered.

Though in my case, the evidence was clear, we are all holding on to misinterpretations from childhood that may not be easy to dispel.

Misinterpretation

Prior to this moment of discovery, if you had asked me to bring up a mental image of myself in the fifth grade, I would have pictured myself as fat, but my impression was inaccurate. I had based my perception on misinformation, namely the teasing of kids in my fifth-grade class.

After this revelation, my sense was that I had seen those pictures before. I wondered why I hadn't *recognized* the inaccuracy of my perception. Why had I hung on to an interpretation of reality that didn't serve me? Why now, many years later, did I suddenly *acknowledge* the inaccuracy in my perception? How many other misinterpretations or misunderstandings had I allowed to skew my perception of myself?

Divorce

To further illustrate misinterpretations, I would like to use the subject of divorce, because it is one of the most common areas of profound misinterpretation. When a child's parents get divorced, misinterpretations tend to run rampant and have lasting effects on that child's perception of reality. The misinterpretations associated with this type of traumatic event often affect a person throughout his life.

A child's misinterpretations around a divorce almost always include a feeling that it was the child's fault. Older children may even intellectually "understand" that the parents had problems that they did not cause, but the charged atmosphere and negativity create emotional confusion and leave deep impressions.

With an emotional crisis, fighting parents often lose their capacity to contain their behavior; they unconsciously blame their children for the marital problems. The child doesn't have the capacity to discern whether the accusation is accurate or not. The child simply internalizes the misinterpretation that he or she *caused* the divorce.

The situation can get even more complicated if the parents manipulate the children and encourage misinterpretation. Hurt parents will often enlist their children in their cause or to take their side. The result is that the child misunderstands the circumstances and ends up with lifelong emotional scars—often bubbling up later as shame, blame, or guilt. A fundamental premise of this work is that all shame, blame, and guilt involve misinterpretations of the past. When past events are viewed accurately, there is nothing to be ashamed or guilty about.

Exercise:

Recognizing Shame and Guilt as Misinterpretations

Note: This is a closed-eye process, so read the directions all the way through one time and then take yourself though the process as best you can. You needn't get this "right"; just do the best you can to remember the exercise.

This exercise will focus mainly on shame or guilt. We will have an opportunity to work with blame later.

At this time, I would like you to close your eyes. Focus on any shame or guilt that you are holding in your body. Localize it to a specific part of your body if you can. You may want to put your hands on the place in your body where you feel the emotions are held. Stay with the feeling as long as possible. If you have visual impressions, try to follow them. This is like unraveling a ball. Your memory may hold on very tightly to an interpretation, but when it starts to unravel, it generally comes apart rather quickly. This is not necessarily about figuring anything out. I just want you to begin to surrender to an underlying understanding of your particular reality. Try to track the events where your misinterpretations (the shame and guilt) were formed. Try to remember (the prefix "re-" and the root "member"—meaning to put back together) the truth about the experience.

When you open your eyes, I want you to set an intention to work consciously to apply compassion to yourself and everyone involved in your situation. Now, identify any misinterpretations that you held previously and that you can now begin to perceive differently. In your journal, identify the circumstances. Recognize the needs of the younger you and have empathy and compassion for yourself as you process the information. Allow the journal to be your confidante as you explore and re-interpret your experience.

Use self-forgiveness to release any residual judgments and embrace the truth about your human experience.

Author's Note: This is courageous work you are doing—you are healing.

7.

The False Self

Getting Personal: Pretending to Be Tough

Even thirty years later, I still feel a little embarrassed by the memory. I believed that looking tough would somehow protect me. There we were—my father and I—at Get's Shopping Center, buying me Ben Davis work pants, Converse All-Star high tops, and T-shirts (black and white only). It was a working-class uniform that suggested I could fight. Today it seems absurd, but at the time, it was very real. I had dressed inappropriately for the type of school I was attending. I had become a target.

I was being bullied and everyone felt helpless: the school, my parents, and everyone involved in my situation were at a loss as to how to stop it. The political and social climate of the public school system in San Francisco in 1976 had everyone confused and overwhelmed.

I was part of the experiment that took middle-class kids and bused them into inner-city schools, and took inner-city kids and bused them into middle-class neighborhoods. The concept at the time was that it might level the playing field and encourage inner-city kids to perform better. The reality was that it profoundly didn't work.

My school was a hybrid—not exactly inner city, but close enough to the "projects" to draw the "intended population" with an added theory of combining fourth, fifth, and sixth graders in the same classroom. The *hypothesis* was that the older kids would help the younger kids learn. The *reality* was that the older kids picked on the younger kids.

Eric and Paul were black and I was white. Eric was in fifth grade, Paul in sixth, and I was in fourth grade. I showed up to school the first day with my blonde hair, cut in a bowl style, plaid bell-bottom pants, and a button-up shirt. My look had "target" written all over it. Eric and Paul greeted me as "White Boy" and began taunting me from the first day of school. Pushing and shoving me in the coat room, tripping me as I walked up the aisle in class, sticking gum in my hair on the playground, and countless other tactics had me completely traumatized.

It is hard to fathom the scene at the time, but there was a lot of racial tension. The Black Panther party was on the nightly news, spewing slogans of hate. Liberal white politicians, teachers, and school administrators were trying to solve issues of inequality with ill-conceived legislation aimed at integrating the schools.

The school administrators met with my parents to try to solve the problem. Their challenge was that nothing they had done was effective in stopping the bullying. They had contacted Eric and Paul's parents; they had suspended them from school. They had done everything short of expelling them, which was not an option—a black activist group had pressured the school board into adopting a policy that prohibited expelling any more black children from school. The bullies could be asked not to come back after the school year was over, but they could not be expelled.

The principal had been the one to suggest the costume. "Perhaps if your son dressed a little tougher, they might leave him alone," he told my father. So there we were at Get's Shopping Center, buying me clothes to try to make me look tougher.

The new clothing didn't work, so my parents ended up taking me out of school and sending me to a local Catholic school.

This was my first experience trying to "construct" a sense of self, but it was not my last experience by any means. Throughout my life, my persona or personality was derived in large part out of defense. I put on a false exterior image to try to feel safe. I wanted to be liked, so I adjusted my clothing and behavior to try to be cool or fit in. I rejected feelings that I associated with being weak. I denied and repressed memories that I didn't know what to do with. When things were painful and confusing growing up, I made up stories to try to make myself feel better about the situation. I developed a false self who denied my authentic experience in an attempt to try to meet my needs for safety, recognition, love, acceptance, etc.

Making Up Stories
We all make up stories to help us feel better about past situations. In the case of divorce (and countless other traumatic events in our childhood), adults unconsciously collude with us in making up stories. Frankly, most adults are still making up stories themselves, because they are still trying to explain and justify their feelings.

The stories we tell may not be true and the authentic part of us knows this. Unraveling the stories and getting to "our truth" is work. But the work is often made harder by the layers and complexity of the stories we have "bought into." We don't only have our personal stories, but we also have our collective stories to sort through.

The Collective Stories

Every tribe (family and society) establishes a firm set of rules for what is acceptable and unacceptable. All of human behavior is characterized as good or bad, right or wrong. Tales are told and history is written from a cultural perspective—representing a collective story. Feelings are also judged as good or bad, right or wrong. There are usually very limited opportunities for socially acceptable expressions of feelings. Naturally our self-perception becomes distorted as we attempt to adjust reality to fit these agreed-upon norms. In simple terms, we want to fit in. We are trying to be successful based on the rules and expectations of our tribe. However, this distortion, this self-denial, ultimately has negative effects.

Truth Often Lies in Feelings

Human beings have needs, and needs evoke feelings. Feelings are messy. Sometimes we try to figure them out, often we try to control them, and still other times we repress them. Rarely are we taught how to appropriately express them. Many feelings are simply "off limits." But feelings hold the key to unlocking "our truth."

Addressing our needs and expressing our feelings is fundamental to healing, because it allows us to embrace our experience. The bottom line when it comes to traumatic events from the past is that it doesn't matter what really happened or who did what to whom; the only thing that really matters is how we experienced the event. No one can argue with feelings when they are framed correctly without shame, blame, or guilt. When we peel away the layers of protection we have formed around a particular event, we begin to discover feelings that have not been resolved. These unresolved feelings and the interpretation (misinterpretation) of these feelings are what create issues. The stories we tell invariably involve judgment—and judgment locks our limiting interpretation in place.

We must unravel the stories we have told and find the truth about ourselves and our experience. We must release judgment as we learn to accept ourselves and others. We must also learn to accept (but not over-identify with) the tribe we come from. We must learn to navigate the rules, expectations, and understanding of the family and society we live in as we search for outlets to express our feelings authentically and get our needs met.

Ongoing Exercise: A Story I've Been Telling

I want you to reserve a handful of pages (just three or so) in your journal. At this point, I just want you to title it, "A Story I've Been Telling." On the first line, start with, "A story I've been telling that no longer serves me is …"

Whenever you feel inspired—or as often as you feel inspired—I want you to finish this sentence. This exercise may become clearer once you have completed the future exercise on "reframing," but feel free to debunk any and all stories that come up, whenever they come up, when they no longer serve you. (Remember: It is always helpful to set an intention before doing an exercise. Even a simple intention, such as "my intention in this exercise is to go for the deepest healing possible," can be effective.)

8.
Expanding Consciousness
with Observation

Getting Personal: Compassion Breeds Compassion

I live a block away from a large medical building in Los Angeles. We moved there because my wife worked on the tenth floor and she could see a corner house for rent from her office. For months, it stayed vacant—waiting for us to move into it, I guess. Anyway, in the lobby of the building is a delightful little bistro owned by a Southern European woman who serves a mixture of Mediterranean and American food. I eat lunch there several times a week.

I arrived to order my standard half-sandwich and soup special, sit by the window, and take a break from work. On this particular day, I noticed a woman slumped over in her chair—it looked like she was sleeping. After some time, there was a bit of commotion as an elderly patron complained about her to the manager. Evidently, this woman had been in the restaurant for some time, and she kept waking up and falling asleep. Others in the restaurant seemed to be reacting to the woman's behavior, in addition to the other patron who complained. The waitress chimed in the complaint conversation, adding that she wanted to take the woman's order, but every time she went over, the woman was asleep. The waitress reported that she had tried several times to wake her up. The manager decided to call the building security.

When the security person arrived, the woman had just woken up. Living in Los Angeles, I just assumed she was drunk or on drugs. I figured the security guard would kick her out of the restaurant. But he didn't. Instead, he sat down with her. He asked her how she was doing. He was patient and kind. Frankly, I was confused. The other patrons seemed confused as well. Why wasn't he hauling her out of the restaurant? Her behavior was clearly offensive. Why should we paying patrons put up with this drunk/stoned/whatever woman disturbing our lunch?

I was curious, so I leaned in and listened. As it turned out, this woman had come to the restaurant after visiting one of the doctor's offices upstairs. She needed to eat something to try to bring her blood sugar up before she went home. She evidently had a severe medical condition that caused her to fall asleep when her blood sugar levels got too low. She needed to eat something, but she couldn't stop falling asleep.

As I sat there and listened to this incredibly compassionate security guard help this woman, I was filled with emotion. He helped her pick the item from the menu that she wanted, then he called over the waitress and ordered. He sat and talked with her while she ate. When she was finished eating and had regained her strength, the security guard helped her back to the building's main lobby to wait for a cab.

Before I left the building, I found that security guard and I told him what a lesson he had taught me. I had been so quick to judge that woman. The way he handled the incident reminded me to have compassion and observe situations from a neutral perspective before drawing a conclusion.

The Conscious Compassionate Observer

Emotional maturity often comes well after a child is declared an adult. Rarely in Western culture is a child raised with a healthy emotional sense of self. The reason is that most adults are still emotionally relating to the world as children. They have not developed what I refer to as a *conscious compassionate observer*.

The conscious compassionate observer is a way of viewing circumstances that allows for a multi-dimensional perspective of situations or events.

It is your conscious compassionate observer that can begin to identify the situations where you react automatically, based on your emotional state or according to the beliefs, stories, and "agreements" of your tribe, family, and peer group.

The emotionally mature adult can take responsibility for his emotional state as well as take into consideration the circumstances surrounding a situation. The emotionally mature adult has individuated from others and can view other people's experience as separate. If a person is upset with him, he has the ability to consider the other person's viewpoint and circumstances (compassion).

Here is a simple illustration of the difference between an emotionally mature adult and a child: If you tell a child that he is stupid, the child will immediately react; perhaps he will cry or scream or call you stupid. The child doesn't have an "observer." On the other hand, the adult with a developed conscious compassionate observer will have cultivated an inner voice that suggests, "Well, I may or may not be stupid. Where is that idea coming from?" The adult would consider why the other person was calling him stupid.

The emotionally mature adult can listen to someone's claims with empathy and compassion for the fact that the person is angry, discern what part might actually be accurate, and differentiate the issues not relating to him personally. The emotionally mature adult is able to identify and take responsibility for the part he or she has played in the situation and may even apologize for his or her role in inducing the anger and frustration.

The emotionally mature adult can see the situation clearly and may be able to offer some suggestions for making amends or resolving the issue.

The emotionally mature adult *does not react,* internally or externally, because the emotionally mature adult recognizes that reactions are always about the person doing the reacting. Often reactions are triggered by past experience and not necessarily about what is happening presently. (We will discuss this more in a later chapter entitled "Reactions Are about the Past.")

Exercise: Take Your Conscious Compassionate Observer Along for the Day

The best way to develop your conscious compassionate observer is to practice using it. The following exercise is designed to help nurture this tool.

What you want to do is be alert (mindful) in all interactions, particularly when you become *annoyed, frustrated, disgusted, or angry.* While some of your senses are responding to outside information, keep an active barometer on the inside and *track* your reactions. In particular, try to look at any situation from the other person's perspective, and *identify* any misinterpretations on your part (or theirs).

Don't try to change or correct your reactions; instead, become like a recorder and enter the most significant observations in your journal. Remember that the goal of the exercise is to have compassion for yourself and others. Every time you witness judgment, it is a clear indication that you have misinterpreted the events. Gently forgive yourself for judging yourself or others and apply a compassionate perspective to the situation.

For example, say you are at the market. You are in the express line, and you begin to feel as if the clerk is taking too long. Perhaps the customer who is checking out is fumbling for ID or writing a check. Try to take note of how and when your mood changes. Recognize if you begin to see yourself as right and some other person or people as wrong. Notice how others are behaving. What are their reactions?

Sometimes it is effective to use an external meter to measure your inner reality. For example, say you were to check your watch and count the actual time you spent waiting. You may find that the check writer only "robbed" you of three minutes of your time. Notice the price you paid for your interpretation that someone was doing something "to you." Track your irritability and how long it takes you to get over your frustration. Does your frustration carry over into your next activity or interaction? Perhaps you find yourself struggling to get out of the parking lot or are caught in traffic once you reach the street. Observe the "snowball effect" as your negativity attracts more negativity.

As you do this exercise, you will find two significant realities: First, how difficult it is to engage in the world and still maintain a conscious compassionate observer; your reactions are so automatic that they overwhelm your perspective as they disturb your peace and distract your attention. Second, as you do this exercise, you will recognize how quickly you fall into negative energy flows as situations that disturb you mount and build one upon the other in your unconscious ("snowball effect"). Please write in your journal about your experience.

9.
Negative Self-perception

Getting Personal: Free to Blossom

I began feeling successful my sophomore year in high school. Prior to that time, I don't remember feeling particularly good about myself for any extended period of time. I believe I began to blossom in large part due to my older brother moving out of the house. My brother didn't just move out of the house; he moved to Germany to be an exchange student for a year—and I began to succeed. My grades went up. I got a part in a school play. I suddenly started making new friends, and girls started taking interest in me.

Growing up, my brother resented me. He looked for every opportunity to put me down. I worked tirelessly to try to prove myself to him, attempting to get him to like me, but it never worked. My brother had an incredibly knack for pointing out my deficiencies. He was bright and he skillfully worded things in a way that triggered my insecurity.

When he left, I felt free and my successes began to build on one another.

The Voice in Your Head

Everyone has had the experience of being around someone they know likes them; their personality comes out in a delightful way, and they feel loose and confident. I had Bob (whom I talked about in an earlier chapter). Conversely, everyone has been around someone they know holds some negative judgment toward them. When they are in this person's presence, they experience themselves as being defensive and feeling awkward. In my case, my brother represented this dynamic.

Growing up, we may not have had the ability to observe the experience. Instead, we reacted by praising the person with whom we felt positive about ourselves, and blamed or bad-mouthed the person with whom we felt negatively about ourselves. We divided the world into two categories: *friends* and *adversaries*. As a defense, we formed very rigid beliefs about ourselves and others. Meanwhile, we unconsciously absorbed criticism and blame from others.

As mentioned in the previous chapter regarding developing an observer, when we become mature adults, we can separate ourselves from others. We recognize that the person isn't actually doing anything "to us," they are simply triggering us. Part of the Service to Self™ process is beginning to track our reactions and beliefs. We want to observe our experience and make conscious choices instead of simply reacting.

Ultimately we want to direct our thoughts so that we focus on the positive part of ourselves and quiet the negative or judgmental part of ourselves as often as possible. We want to explore our beliefs and opinions to determine which ones serve us and are in our best interest and which ones we may want to release and dispel. This leads to a greater sense of well-being.

When no one is around, we can begin to become conscious of what side of ourselves we are "being" with. Are we being with the side of ourselves that is judging us rather than the side of ourselves that is loving and accepting us? In this chapter, we will explore the negative relationship we have with ourselves and the beliefs that perpetuate our negative self-perception.

Where Negative Self-perception Comes From

In our culture, we spend a lot of time and energy focusing on our own deficiencies. Growing up, a lot of things are pointed out in negative terms. Those whose intent may have been to help us or spare us potential pain often used negative feedback to attempt to teach us.

If you grew up in Western culture, I am sure you experienced your share of negative feedback. In school, there were always a lot of red pen marks on your paper, but in all likelihood, there weren't a lot of encouraging remarks. The adults in your life (whose job it was to help and teach you) often used criticism and shame. The peers in your life (who themselves were being put down) were probably merciless. Your experience supports a negative self-perception. From this point of view, you may find yourself comparing yourself to others, or to some imagined idea of perfection; as a result, you never felt "good" enough.

Our media culture exacerbates this problem by creating images of beauty and success that are virtually unattainable. Capitalism thrives on insecurity. The premise is that if companies can make you feel insecure as a way of promoting products, you become a much better consumer because they convince you that their product will make you feel better about yourself.

The image most of us have of an ideal body may be an unhealthy, under-weight, body that we should not be trying to emulate. The women we see on the cover of fashion magazines are usually underweight. Women, specifically, need to maintain a certain amount of body fat to be healthy. Many of us have a skewed perception where we see deficiencies based on an unrealistic and unhealthy ideal.

It is important to shift from seeing deficiencies to seeing strengths. We all need to learn to lead with our strengths. The truth is that when we lead with our strengths, the deficiencies often disappear or become much less important.

But if we focus our energy on what we are *not,* then these perceptions tend to dominate our consciousness and pull us down into mediocrity and insecurity. When someone is confident and talented, they attract positive people—and positive results—to themselves.

How often have you met someone who you thought was not that interesting, but then after talking to them, you found yourself totally engaged and thoroughly attracted to that person? How many talented musicians or actors are considered sexy even though they don't match the cultural ideal of what makes someone beautiful?

The opposite is also true: How many times have you seen someone you thought was physically attractive, but after talking to them for a short time, you became uninterested?

The Service to Self™ process is designed to help support your gifts, talents, and abilities; as you work to dispel negative self-perception, you will learn to lead with your strengths.

Irrational Beliefs, Limiting Beliefs, and Negative Self-talk

In order to overcome negative self-perception, it is important to confront some of the unconscious habits that sustain your negative self-image. There is something I call "chatter," which goes on in your mind, and it is usually fueled by irrational and limiting beliefs. This habitual chatter is also referred to as negative self-talk. The Service to Self™ process is designed to identify some of the root causes of negative self-talk and reverse their effect using positive self-talk.

Irrational Beliefs

Irrational beliefs are generally rooted in fear. Superstition is a good example of an irrational belief. Your rational mind knows that stepping on a crack, walking under a ladder, or breaking a mirror will not result in some negative effect on your life. However, you may still avoid stepping on cracks, walking under ladders, or breaking mirrors out of an irrational fear.

Limiting Beliefs

A good example of a limiting belief comes from an earlier story. At the beginning of this book, I told the story about the woman who felt she needed to lose twenty more pounds. As it turned out, this woman was once a model. In modeling school, she had been told that based on her height, she should never be more than 125 pounds.

During one of our sessions, I asked her about the number she had in her head: 125. I wanted to know where she believed the modeling school instructor had gotten it. She quickly responded that he worked with models all the time, and he obviously knew what an appropriate weight should be for a woman her height. But as we talked further and examined this assumption, my client admitted that the information could very well have been pulled from thin air.

She reported having taken the modeling classes more than thirty years ago, and ever since then, she had held that imaginary number in her head. She reported countless experiences over the past three decades of getting on the scale and feeling horrible about being over 125 pounds. Interestingly, she admitted that the few times she actually weighed 125 pounds, good friends and family told her that she looked too skinny. All of these years, this single limiting belief had caused an immeasurable amount of suffering.

Exercise: Tracking Unconscious Beliefs (an ongoing exercise)
Tracking is a way of making the unconscious conscious. You are beginning this inventory now, but will be adding to it throughout the process. For this exercise, you may want to use a computer, or you can write this out by hand in your journal. If you use a journal, please leave at least ten pages in order to add to this list as the process continues.

First, set an intention. Then open a document (or your personal journal) and begin to list irrational or limiting beliefs that you are aware you hold. You may find yourself hesitant to admit to some of the beliefs because your rational mind "knows better." Even if only 10 percent of you "buys into" the irrational or limiting belief, write it down.

Don't be concerned if you can't think of any or only come up with a few. The fact is that you may not be consciously aware of these types of beliefs. However, as the process continues, you're likely to uncover many of them.

10.
Programming and Agreements

Getting Personal: Catholic Guilt

I grew up in a Catholic culture. My parents were not strict Catholics, by any means. In fact, they were relatively "lapsed" Catholics who only went to church periodically. Still, I was baptized, did my first communion, attended a Catholic school from fifth grade on, served as an altar boy, etc.

My parents both felt betrayed by their religion. Catholicism of the 1940s and 1950s had instilled a heavy burden of guilt in their minds. The cultural revolution of the 1960s (along with dramatic changes in the Catholic Church following Vatican II) left my parents (and many others) rethinking their relationship with the church. My parents learned to question church teaching. With strict rules suddenly turned upside down, my parents began to make up their own minds about what was wrong and what was right for them in their lives.

My parents felt as if they had been brainwashed. And my parents didn't want my brother and me to be conditioned by the same types of teaching. Despite their liberation, the concept of heaven and hell had been etched into their minds to the point where both of my parents report feeling horrible guilt for using contraception or "breaking" some other church rule they were choosing not to abide by.

I am grateful to my parents for their intention to spare me the pain of the profound misinterpretation of Jesus's message. I recognize their attempts to teach me an alternate perspective, to counteract the messages I was exposed to in Catholic grammar school. I would like to report that I didn't experience any guilt growing up in a Catholic culture, but that would not be true. The fact is that my cultural heritage is laden with subtle messages about wrong and right and heaven and hell. I did not escape the burden of guilt.

Today, I feel grateful for the many enlightened priests and teachers I encountered in my high school and college years at Jesuit schools. There is a profound distinction between the theology of the Jesuits and mainstream Catholic teaching. Despite this counteractive force, I have still had to work very hard to dispel the powerful indoctrination I inadvertently absorbed growing up in a traditional Catholic culture.

Collective Beliefs

In the previous chapter on irrational or limiting beliefs, we discussed how experiences from our personal histories can lead to beliefs. Beyond experiences, many irrational and limiting beliefs stored in our unconscious minds come from programming.

We are born to a particular family, a particular race, and a particular culture. We come from a particular country and we participate in a particular religion. We are born and raised to follow a particular structure of beliefs. Early on in life, we begin assimilating into the identifying beliefs of our particular tribe.

Our underlying conditioning binds us to a number of different agreements. We agree about what is right and what is wrong. We learn family and cultural expectations. We come to understand what traits our tribe considers positive and what characteristics our people see as negative. We agree on how men are supposed to act, or how women are supposed to act.

When we witness a culture that does not agree with our rules and norms, we often consider that group aberrant or wrong. What we don't recognize is simply that they have a different set of agreements.

Many of our families have specific roles that each member is "cast" in. For instance, the oldest girl may be expected to stay in the home and take care of the elders, while the oldest boy is expected to marry and bear grandchildren. These types of agreements are spoken about in code. They are understood silently and often secretively.

Then there are subtle agreements stored in the subconscious. These are usually born out of family dysfunction, traumatic events, or difficult situations; these agreements can profoundly limit us. These types of agreements are often referred to as "family secrets." These agreements affect our sense of self. If we internalized negative feedback as children, we usually have made some sort of agreement with ourselves and others.

Operating Assumptions

Our agreements are like operating assumptions. Everyone has them, but no one knows precisely which ones are in effect. Differences may become apparent when we interact with people from another race or religion. Sometimes we unconsciously look to align ourselves with people who look like us or practice the same religion because we feel a common bond (the energy of shared agreements).

In the case of race or religion, common agreements can be pretty easy to detect. But often, we unconsciously find other members of our tribe whose subconscious agreements match ours. This is why people who were abused as children find an abuser as a mate. Many people who share common family patterns find one another and act out the same pattern all over again.

It is important to become aware of your agreements; they can profoundly affect the choices you make in your life.

Tracking Our Agreements

Becoming authentic requires you to have a sense of your agreements. You must be consciously willing to "break" agreements that are not serving you, as well as make agreements, understanding what you are choosing, and being willing to deal with whatever ramifications follow this type of conscious choice. The following definitions of the three types of agreements will help you better understand this concept.

Three Levels of Agreement

- **Conscious Agreements:** Making agreements and following through on those agreements is part of being in integrity. This is commonly referred to as "being a person of your word." As you begin to *acknowledge* your talents, gifts, and abilities, you will need to make conscious choices to find outlets and forms of expression for those attributes. Becoming clear and making conscious agreements will propel you into definite courses of action that will *support* the realization of your potential.

- **Unconscious Agreements Based on Assumptions:** Besides conscious agreements, agreements can also be made unconsciously. Some of these agreements we call assumptions, and that reminds us of a famous saying: "When you assume, you make an *ass* out of *you* and *me*." Assumptions are very unhealthy types of agreements because, in fact, they are based on unsubstantiated understandings. There is an inherent lack of clarity in assumptions that invariably leads to negative consequences.

  Working to be clear is a challenge that a lot of people are not very good at. There are a lot of reasons for this, including wanting to be liked, not wanting to disappoint others, trying to say or do the "right" thing, not wanting to commit oneself, and so on and so on. Moving toward clarity involves taking responsibility and asking for what you want while holding yourself and others accountable for any lack of clarity that gets in the way of you becoming the "you" you were born to be.

- **Unconscious Tribal Agreements:** There is another type of unconscious agreement that is very prevalent but rarely discussed, stemming from unspoken rules. They pertain to many types of group affiliation including culture, race, and socioeconomic status. They can be fostered by parents, society, school, and the media. These unconscious agreements have incredible power over the human psyche and are often elusive and hard to identify. Another word for these types of agreements is "inheritance"—which suggests that they have been passed down *to* you rather than having been chosen *by* you. However, if you are going to be free to live up to your potential, it is important that you have a sense of the agreements you may have unconsciously made—and their effects on your life.

Expectation and Entitlement

Expectation and entitlement are beliefs that are born out of agreements. For example, a woman may have certain expectations about a husband. She may marry a man without ever knowing consciously that she expects certain things. Several years into the marriage, she may find herself resentful of her husband for things she unconsciously believes he should be doing. Similarly, that same man has a laundry list of expectations and things he feels entitled to. Many divorces are not really about the things that the couple make the separation about, but are really linked to unconscious expectations and entitlement.

Getting Personal: Men Are Disappointments

A longtime friend of mine keeps finding herself in relationships with men who disappoint her. After tracking some family patterns, she has come to recognize a similar story that most of the women in her family share: "Men are disappointments." In a recent conversation, she told me, "It is as if my disappointment in men has a life of its own." She was conscious that she projected disappointment onto men and she was unsure if any man could escape the story that was running in her head. I suggested that she might want to examine the unconscious agreement the women in her family seem to have made about men, then do the work to break the agreement she has bought into in the future.

Exercise: Agreements Inventory
Again, leave additional pages in your journal, as you may find yourself coming back to this inventory and adding to it in the future. Based on your understanding of agreements, please *track* your experience of the following and write about it in your journal:

What assumptions do you find yourself operating on that may be erroneous?

Are there any unconscious agreements that might challenge you going for what you want? (For example: "If I succeed, who am I going to betray?")

Are you afraid to ask questions? If so, of whom?

What are the cultural expectations of you as a man/woman? (e.g. "A man should ..." or "A woman should ...")

Do you have unconscious agreements about food or weight?

Please list any other agreements you are presently aware of or uncover as you continue doing the Service to Self™ process.

11.
Sitting in Discomfort and Giving Upset a Voice

Getting Personal: Getting Sick in Order to Heal

I hate being sick. I especially hate the stomach flu and food poisoning. I really don't like to vomit. Physiologically, vomiting serves a purpose—to expel toxins from the body in order to promote healing.

Recently, I caught the stomach flu. Once I recognized that I was sick, I set the intention to surrender and allow the illness to help me release and to teach me. It was an amazing experience.

Three aspects of this illness struck me as profound. The first pertains to my resistance to vomiting. In order to gain some relief, I understood I needed to vomit. Every time I vomited, I felt better, but I resisted vomiting, thereby extending my nausea. This relates to my experience of withholding around my feelings. I tend to hold them in, even though I recognize that expressing them will make me feel better.

The second part of the illness that struck me was a feeling of vulnerability. I watched the movie *The Kid* while I was sick, and found myself crying profusely. My defenses were down, and I connected deeply with the characters in the movie—my vulnerability allowed me to be "touched" by the film. This made me feel deeply alive and inspired. It reminded me what a tremendous gift my vulnerability is.

The third aspect of the illness that was powerful to me revolved around my recovery. As I began to feel better, I felt tremendous gratitude for my health. I really enjoy feeling grateful. It seems to open up my world, and everything becomes a little bit brighter and more special.

The experience of being sick and allowing myself to go through the experience consciously was a wonderful opportunity and gift.

Embracing Discomfort as Your Teacher

Now that you understand the concept of the conscious compassionate observer, and you recognize some of the beliefs and agreements that operate in your unconscious mind, it is time to address discomfort and upset. For those of us who have struggled with weight, discomfort and upset are easily masked or suppressed with comfort food. Food is part of a coping mechanism that we have used to deal with uncomfortable situations.

The Service to Self ™ process suggests that by "sitting" in discomfort, you can allow it to be your teacher rather than denying or avoiding the feelings by stuffing them down with food. The discomfort (similar to nausea when you are sick) is present for a reason.

Sitting in the discomfort and giving upset a voice are major keys to changing behavior. When you experience discomfort, you must learn to interrupt the unconscious patterns of behavior by observing the feelings. Expressing the feelings relieves the tension that is held in your body and/or mind; it allows you to apply compassion and perspective to the situation that is associated with your upset. Again, you are working to make the unconscious conscious.

In order to experience a shift, it is not enough to just understand your feelings intellectually. You must create some outlet for experiencing and expressing your feelings. For our purposes, your journal will serve as a repository for expressing emotions.

Exercise: Add "Checking In" to Your Process

Most people deal with the discomfort that arises in life by "checking out" - unconscious eating is a way of checking out. This book suggests that the way to change the unhealthy patterns in your life requires awareness, or "checking in." You must develop an inner observer who can view situations with some objectivity. This will allow you to make conscious choices instead of reacting unconsciously.

It is important to get your feelings out. This part of the process will develop as you continue to read this book and continue to develop your personal process. For now, however, it is just important to explore your feelings in a safe and healthy way. At this point, it is not terribly important that you be "charged" with emotion when you do this exercise. I simply want you to explore and develop another tool to use as you continue on this journey toward self-acceptance, self-appreciation, and self-love.

The goal of this exercise is to probe your feelings. Be very conscious of any tendency to assign blame (to others or to yourself). This does not mean that you cannot be mad at someone or sad because of something that occurred. It simply means to stay away from complex explanations of who or what is to blame. Just report your feelings and focus on your inner world. The story about what happened is not important; only use the story to get to the feelings. You just want to explore your feelings.

Now, don't stop or think that you are doing it wrong if judgments and "story" find their way into this process. This is a stream-of-consciousness process where it is important just to let the words flow onto the page (or screen) without editing. If you find yourself going into a story or explanation, just gently come back to your feelings. YOU CANNOT GET THIS PROCESS WRONG.

If you are having trouble expressing your feelings, that may be important information to know about yourself. If you find yourself feeling like you need to explain or justify your feelings, then that may be important information to know about yourself.

This process can be repeated often—the more resistance you have to it, the more you may want to do it. Your feelings need a voice. You are simply learning to explore your feelings so that you can begin to embrace your experience and apply compassion and deeper understanding to your own humanity.

Utilize this process in the future when your discomfort is especially amplified to assist you in moving through it.

Find a quiet time and place to work this process.

Center yourself by closing your eyes and breathing in and out slowly and deeply. Connect with your inner authority and call on it to support you in allowing your feelings to come out. Set an intention to give your feelings a voice. Then ask yourself, "How am I feeling?" If you know of a particular trigger that is present for you, go ahead and explore it. Examples of this may be recent situations at work that upset you, or an ongoing disagreement you are having with a loved one. Once you have tapped into some feeling, open your eyes and use your stream of consciousness to explore your feelings. Write for ten minutes without stopping—no matter what comes out. Just remember that your intention is to give your feelings a voice.

12.
Reactions Are About the Past

Getting Personal: "It's not about asparagus."

"You cook them for five minutes," I told her.

"No," she snapped back, "ten minutes, I'm sure of it."

"Okay," I replied, "but they are going to be mushy."

"Why can't you just let me do it my way?" she asked. "Why must you always control me?" she continued in an angry tone.

"Why can't I have an opinion without it being a personal attack on you?" I shot back.

It was the start of the first big fight my current wife Jasmine and I ever had. Even though we had been dating for more than six months, the stress of recently moving in together was triggering emotional issues.

Josh, my stepson, was ten years old at the time, and he was clearly shaken as the argument escalated. That evening, we both put Josh to bed. He was upset and confused. "Why are you guys fighting about asparagus?" he asked.

"It's not about asparagus," I told him.

Jasmine and I knew enough to know the fight had nothing to do with asparagus. We assured Josh that we would talk it through, that we were committed to being together and raising him. We explained that sometimes, adults get upset and angry and that there is an opportunity for people in intimate relationships to heal past hurts and become happier, healthier people—but the healing can be hard work.

The truth about that evening was that we had both been married before, and a lot of fear based on past experience was coming up. Jasmine was wary of being controlled. I felt like I was being punished for having an opinion. Thankfully, Jasmine and I had some decent communication skills and a wonderful resource in our friends Joyce and Andre Patenaude. Joyce and Andre are Imago Relationship Counselors in Santa Monica, California, and they helped us work through the issue.

When Jasmine and I fight, we recognize that it is rarely about the initial topic or trigger, and almost always about something deeper. Our relationship has become a safe place to work through issues, heal, and grow.

Josh is now nineteen and he has a girlfriend. When they are fighting, he often uses the expression, "It's not about asparagus."

> Intimate relationships provide a sacred classroom where each of us is offered the opportunity to learn and grow from the intense challenges that every couple must face.

Feelings and the Past

Now that you have begun to explore your feelings, we are going to discuss how feelings get triggered so that you can be more compassionate with yourself out in the world.

When a person reacts, he or she is often responding from the past rather than the present. The present circumstances are a *trigger* for emotions locked in past experiences.

When we were children, our parents were responsible for responding to our emotions. Very few parents were clear about their emotions, so they were not well equipped to help us deal with ours. Contemporary psychology has formulated the concept of the inner child.* The idea is that each of us has within us a child whose feelings were cut off or dismissed, based on our early experience with emotions. The adult, who was wounded as a child, doesn't know how to interpret and deal with emotion appropriately. Inner child work involves an inner dialogue with the young part of oneself in order to heal past events.

Such a dialogue is intended to help the adult process emotions that never got expressed when they were children. Inner child work is a means of releasing pent-up feelings, re-interpreting past events, and allowing current emotions an appropriate outlet. This

---

* John Bradshaw is best known for using the expression "inner child." His groundbreaking books outline the concept of the inner child in detail.

type of work can help adults be more effective in expressing their present emotional experience. It can also assist them in becoming less easily triggered.

An Important Distinction

Inner child work does not necessarily require regression. Some people (including many therapists) believe that a person must re-experience traumatic events in order to heal them. Having done quite a bit of regression work, I am not totally convinced that this type of process is necessary. I believe simply relating to one's vulnerability—the child part who didn't know how to deal with the feelings coming up, while localizing the feelings in the body—can help heal misperceptions.

Note: I often discuss locating one's feelings in one's body, but I don't necessarily explain why this is important. Listed in the appendix, you will find some fascinating work by doctors and scientists (such as Dr. Peter Levine) that go into vast detail about how feelings are localized and stored in various parts of the body. Dr. Candace Pert, in her book, *Molecules of Emotion,* outlines cutting-edge scientific studies that track how emotions are actually stored in the body.

What modern neuroscientists, progressive doctors (specializing in integrated medicine), and psychologists have recently embraced has been known by Chinese and Eastern medicine and philosophy for centuries—that trauma is not necessarily stored in the brain (which is not the sole location of the mind), but rather in specific areas of the body (sometimes known as chakras, centers, or meridians).

This also prompts me to encourage anyone embarking on this process to try to include body work, therapeutic massage, and/or acupuncture as a regular routine if at all possible, to *release* pent-up emotions in tension points that professionals in these fields can locate and "work out."

Your Defense System

Your inner child represents the vulnerable part of you that you may well have tried to protect or deny for many years. However, your defenses—intended to keep you safe—may be costing you a great deal energetically. Defensive personas are inherently inauthentic but also ineffective in truly protecting you. Underneath your hard exterior is a vulnerable person who experiences every slight, every rejection, and every unkind word.

In this process, you will start to develop the capacity for self-acceptance that will begin to comfort the inner child (so that food, for example, will become fuel for a new you that you appreciate and care for, instead of comfort for denied or rejected emotions that previously had no outlet or expression).

When you have developed a new sense of personal identity, born out of an inner authority, it no longer becomes essential or even useful to re-experience past traumas. You needn't examine the exact source of misinterpretations in order to experience your feelings and release any shame, blame, or guilt associated with them. You will begin to recognize triggers and observe the sensation (a flush of emotion) without doing anything to change or fix it, simply by having compassion for your own humanity.

Judging Your Emotions

Not only does being defensive cost you energetically, expressing emotions inappropriately costs you as well. Emotions are connected to your life force and creativity. When people are emotionally "shut down," there is very little life force in them. They have unplugged a major part of themselves. As mentioned earlier, feelings are messy and most people have learned to try to avoid them. But resisting and judging your emotions will not make them go away.

Emotions that are not expressed get "bottled up" and internalized, while emotions that are expressed inappropriately lead to shame, blame, and guilt. Unhealthy expressions of emotions along with internalized emotions result in negative behavior patterns – especially around food. In order to change those patterns, we must look at the underlying beliefs a person has about himself as it relates to his emotions. We must develop in ourselves a new emotional sense of self that interrupts the shame, blame, and guilt patterns—and *reframes* situations using a more healthy perspective.

Moving Past Self-judgment

If you look back at past situations, even revisit them in a therapy setting, then view them with compassion for yourself and anyone else involved in the situation, you can do a lot of healing of these memories. As I mentioned earlier, the problem with much contemporary therapy is that it focuses on re-experiencing events without healing them. The release of energy feels good but doesn't last. What is needed is the observation of our judgment of these events—our frequent misinterpretation.

Because of our judgments, we create stories. The stories lock our perceived limitations in place, while acceptance, compassion, and forgiveness are left by the wayside.

Exercise: Tracking Past Hurt and Applying Compassion

Set an intention to heal your memories. Think of an event that occurred in childhood that you still feel a charge about. In your mind's eye, go back in time and remember as much as you can about the experience. In your journal, report the feelings; you don't need to report the events or re-experience the incident, just explore the feelings as if they were occurring in the present moment (e.g., "I feel sad," or "I feel scared"). Now I want you to bring in the voice of the adult you, and give the child inside some feedback. Help her sort out her feelings; tell her it was not her fault.

Once you have applied compassion and wisdom to your past experience, I want you to release any residual shame, blame, or guilt through self-forgiveness. Just put your hands on your heart and say, "I forgive myself for judging myself as …" Keep saying this sentence (filling in the specific judgment you are forgiving) until you feel complete.

Remember the phrase, "and the truth is …" as it can help you apply compassion to yourself and allow you the wisdom that comes from embracing your experience and learning and growing from it.

13.
Reframing

"Think Different"

"Think different" was the grammatically incorrect but highly effective ad campaign for Apple Computers a few years ago. That company understood that by reshaping the perception of its product and crediting its (potential) users with the ability to apply creative ways to *reframe* their own reality, their product and software would enjoy a more substantial value proposition.

You can begin to "think different," and the value proposition for your life is substantial as well.

Utilizing Reframing as a Tool

Reframing is an incredible tool. It serves as a way to re-interpret past events, but it can also have an incredible effect on one's present experience. Simply put, you are going to be practicing viewing things differently. Ultimately, this will have a direct effect on how you view food, you body, and the world around you.

So far, in this book, you have come to understand that your interpretation of reality is tainted by your past. Hopefully you *acknowledge* that beliefs profoundly affect your perception. I like to say, "what you believe is what you perceive." You have worked with the concept of conscious compassionate observer, leading to the cultivation of an inner authority, whom you can call upon to gain insight into situations.

With these concepts clearly understood, you have the opportunity to work with reframing.

Getting Personal: From Burden to Opportunity

The following illustration of reframing seems incredibly simple, but it has had a powerful and lasting effect on one of my clients. She and I have been working on "calling on her observer" and making choices in the moment when she experiences "upset" (interrupting an observed negative reaction followed by a pattern of behavior).

This particular event began when she installed a new program onto her computer and it wasn't performing correctly. She fiddled with it for more than two hours before calling the technical support number in the user's guide. She was already frustrated when the service person answered the call. She recalled feeling like the experience was becoming a huge inconvenience.

She told me that she was short and rude as she relayed the problem to the man, who was going to try to help her through the issue:

> I felt the anxiety rising inside of me as I explained my 'problem' to the tech support person. Then I heard your [me, the author] voice in my head saying that my reactions are about me. I called on my observer

and I began to view the situation very differently. I recognized the irrational belief that the company was in some way responsible for the fact that their program didn't load properly on **my** computer. I wanted someone to blame for the situation, and the nice man working in tech support was the person I chose to take my frustration out on.

As he began trying to help me, I initially dwelled on my puzzlement. Some part of me took the position that the program was flawed and I didn't want to give up my position. I let my confusion continue to fuel my upset. But there was a part inside of me, that the Service to Self™ process had nurtured, that was observing the situation. This observing part was suggesting that I was acting 'crazy.'

But still, I did not want to give up my original position—I was attached to the belief that the program setup was confusing and it 'shouldn't be.'

The tech support advisor was remaining calm; I'm sure he deals with this type of behavior often. I asked him to hold on for one minute and I moved the phone away from my mouth and did the clearing breaths exercise [coming later in the book]. I dropped into my inner authority and I asked that part of me for help in *reframing* this situation.

Suddenly it occurred to me that I had been looking for a computer class to take, because I felt like I really didn't understand my computer. In fact, these types of situations—where I would not know how to navigate the programs on my computer—were frequent. I recognized that maybe this could become an *opportunity* to learn something.

When I picked up the phone again, I apologized for being rude and explained to the man that I really didn't know computers very well. He was incredibly kind and understanding. He assured me that we would figure it out. For over two hours, he stayed on the phone with me. He explained all kinds of different things to me about my computer. He went way beyond the scope of simply getting the program installed.

For the first time ever, I felt like I understood my computer and how it works. Meanwhile I was 'working my process,' and gaining great benefit from using my newly learned skills.

I negotiated with the part of me that had held on to the story I told about not being 'good' with computers. I recognized that as a 'limiting belief' and I opened up to a whole new perception of myself. When we were finished, I felt so much more competent than I had before. I thanked him for helping me, and he gave me a direct extension to call back if I had more questions.

My initial story was based on my reaction, supporting my desire to blame someone for my upset: I was wasting valuable time trying to solve a problem that should never have occurred, and the company was at fault because their software was confusing.

The reframe: I realized that I had been blessed with a two-hour private computer coaching session with one of the most knowledgeable and understanding people I could ever have encountered."

Exercise: Reframing

This exercise is about reframing by calling on your inner support. Close your eyes and access that kind and compassionate voice. You can always call in your mentor or ally who entered your life at a special point and lifted you up by seeing your potential. As I have mentioned, I often use Bob—I literally speak to him as if he were with me.

Now share a situation with your inner support that is challenging or perceived as difficult. Perhaps there is some circumstance that is similar to my client's situation above; perhaps you have blamed (or are prepared to blame) someone else for a wrong that you perceive has been done to you.

Check in with your advisor and see if you get a response that enables you to see the situation from another perspective. First, perhaps you can take the point of view of your perceived adversary; how does it feel to be in that person's skin? What challenges might they be facing?

Then, ask your inner supporter to help you *reframe* your experience from a place of compassion and look for the learning opportunities in what you may have previously regarded as negative.

If appropriate, do an experiment. If the situation is still active in your life, take this point of view into the relationship or circumstances. (It is really okay if this is too much of a stretch; I will introduce another skill later in the book called the "care-fronting dialogue," which allows you to bring the Service to Self™ process directly into your real-life challenges).

Alternatively, you may choose to look back on a previous experience and try to relive it from your new perspective. Continue to energetically send compassion (by holding the intention to understand) to the others who may have been involved, as well as to yourself.

In your journal, dialogue with your inner supporter in response to the negative voices you uncovered in the exercise. *Acknowledge* and *celebrate* yourself for becoming able to reframe a challenging situation. Show appreciation for your inner advisor for his or her wisdom and remind yourself to draw upon this resource again should another difficult occasion arise.

14.

Internalizing and Projection

Getting Personal: Ashamed and Angry

"You're breath smells yucky, Papa!" my four-year-old son Antonio blurted out, when I went to hug him as he was just getting out of bed one morning.

"Sorry," I replied. My feelings were hurt.

"Papa smells stinky," he continued.

Suddenly I got mad. "Antonio, let's go!" I shouted. "It's time to get dressed and eat your breakfast."

"Ahhhh!" he screamed. "You're stinky."

"Let me take care of him," my wife offered.

"Fine, but I don't like that kind of talk," I said as I shot Antonio an angry look.

Shortly after my wife had him dressed, he entered the kitchen, where I was toasting cheddar-cheese-and-onion bagels.

"It smells yucky!" he screamed.

"You don't have to eat it," I snapped back.

"Throw it out, it's stinky! I hate it!" he wailed.

The frustration in my eyes told my wife that she would be the appropriate parent to deal with him. She offered to have him eat in the dining room rather than the kitchen. Ultimately, this seemed like our best solution.

From that day forward, morning after morning, Antonio complained about yucky smells. Morning after morning, Antonio ate in the dining room. It was hard to deal with, and I was particularly short-tempered because it almost always included the statement, "Papa is stinky."

On a few occasions, I felt so angry that some part of me actually wanted to hit my son. That shocked me and made me step back, take a breath, and reconsider the situation. Why was this so upsetting?

In a clear moment, I knew that I would never hit Antonio, because I understood that my reaction was about me. Punishment without some direct correlation to a transgression can be abusive. Discipline comes from the word *disciple,* which means "to teach." But even discipline didn't seem appropriate. I didn't feel coherent enough to try to teach Antonio anything.

Finally, we decided to get an outside opinion. After evaluating my over-the-top reaction, I considered the possibility that perhaps what I perceived as annoying was the result of something I didn't understand. I needed more information.

We consulted an occupational therapist, who suggested that our son may be sensory defensive. After answering a barrage of questions and some testing, the diagnosis was confirmed: Antonio was indeed sensory defensive.

Sensory defensiveness is a condition where a child reacts negatively and intensely to sensory input that would be considered unobjectionable or non-irritating to "neurotypical" children. It is not uncommon for children (especially toddlers) to have a few mild sensory defensive traits. However, when multiple defensive traits impacting the person's day-to-day life are present, that person is considered to be sensory defensive.

Thankfully, Antonio's case was considered mild (as it only occurred in the mornings, and he was generally a very happy, well-rounded child all other times of the day). As it turned out, Antonio's brain had trouble "organizing" when he first woke up in the morning. His perception of smell in particular was especially "disorganized," and anything with a strong odor would set him off. Once we understood the facts behind his behavior, we made adjustments, such as him eating in the dining room. The specialist explained that Antonio might need some help learning to self-regulate when he was feeling the effects of disorganization in his brain. We also began Wilbarger Therapressure Protocol, a massage program, to help him with sensory input.

Today, Antonio is so much less reactive in the mornings, and when he is having trouble, the family simply adjusts; he is given his own space to get centered and allow time for his brain to organize. We are helping him ask for what he needs, rather than lash out. We explain that we understand how sensitive he is to smell in the morning, while stressing that it is not all right to lash out or verbally assault others.

Stepping back and re-evaluating a situation can lead us to a higher and more complete perspective. But there is an important lesson in this experience for me. My reactions are powerful, and perspective can be hard to get hold of when I get emotionally triggered. What part of me was experiencing Antonio as offensive—or more importantly, what part of me got offended? And why did I get so angry? The answer lies in understanding internalizing and projection.

Understanding Internalizing and Projection

If a four-year-old with very little social filtering capability tells you that "your breath is stinky"—taken purely as information, you may want to brush your teeth. But, if you find yourself flushed with shame and anger (as I did), then the comment matched some part in you that feels ashamed and angry. You have been triggered and you are internalizing someone else's reaction.

This is when having an observer can be very beneficial; if you fundamentally know that having bad breath in the morning is normal, their comment doesn't hurt, it simply provides information that you may or may not choose to act on. When the data includes an intense aversion to cheese-and-onion bagels, it may be prudent to consider that the child doing the smelling may have issues independent of the identified irritant. In other words, with a healthy observer, you know that their reaction is about them—not necessarily an inherent nastiness in the smells they are complaining about. In fact, to add to the story I just told, in consulting my wife about my breath, she told me she never noticed my breath being terribly bad in the morning. Clearly, I was taking Antonio's reaction personally; I was internalizing the comment and projecting anger back at Antonio, based on my hurt feelings.

The interesting part of this saga is that the upset often lasted for some time. I found myself being grumpy with my wife, eating breakfast unconsciously, getting into road rage conflicts on the way to drop the kids off at school, etc.

We are all projecting and internalizing. The adjustment is to develop an observer—to understand that our reactions are about us. Conversely, other people's reactions are about them. Understanding this principle can change one's life.

When we project, we are unconsciously looking for people or circumstances to reflect our reality back to us. Shifting to compassion for ourselves and others requires making the unconscious conscious. When we begin to observe ourselves and track our reactions, we have a wonderful opportunity to heal, grow and release weight. We can learn to interrupt negative patterns around food based on reactions that are fueled by upset.

Exercise:
Tracking Your Reactions (projecting and internalizing)
Over the next few days, I want you to track your reactions as much as possible. Write the title "Tracking My Reactions" in

your journal and give yourself about ten pages. In the evening (or during the day if you have time), track reactions you had during the day. Write about what happened and explore your interpretation (e.g., the part of you that reacted and the story you told yourself or others about why you were upset). Note: All situations where you find yourself blaming someone else are opportunities for tracking projection. All situations where your feelings get hurt are opportunities for observing how you internalize things. You "are taking on someone else's projection" or you "are taking something personally." Try not to draw any conclusions from the incidents. This is not a time to judge or try to fix anything—just report your experience.

All Human Behavior Makes Sense

If you knew everyone's life story since birth, you might understand a little bit more about why they behave the way that they do. It may help to know even more history; perhaps you would need to know their family's complete story, back many generations. Maybe you would need to know information about the makeup of their DNA or the chemicals that operate in their brains. At some point, if you had enough information, you would understand why they behave the way that they do. But you don't have all of that information, and frankly, you don't need it—all you need to understand is that all of human behavior "makes sense."

It is often easier to have compassion for a three- or four-year-old than it is to have compassion for adults. Somehow we see little children as innocent. We recognize that they are doing the best they can. They don't scream or cry for no reason. There is an explanation for their upset, even if they can't tell us what it is.

Even if you can have compassion for other adults, it is hard to have compassion for yourself. Many of us carry the belief that we "ought to know better." Compassion for ourselves doesn't come easily; we must practice. In this book, I have tried to provide exercises and tools to practice self-compassion. For me, it is a daily challenge, but one that I am fully committed to; when I "beat myself up," I tend to turn toward food for comfort. Self-compassion is a key element in releasing weight.

15.
Victim Consciousness

Getting Personal: "Don't Disrespect Me"

I volunteer at an organization called Homeboy Industries. Homeboy is a recovery program for ex-gang members and former criminals. It provides jobs, counseling, mentoring, tattoo removal, education, and many other services to help its clients get back on their feet. I teach the Service to Self™ process in a group format once a week, and occasionally lead weekend retreats. Truthfully, it is often a hard place to work. I see dramas played out that are almost automatically programmed by conditioned patterns. These conditioned-response patterns prevent many of the young people from escaping their old neighborhoods and dysfunctional habits, which lands many of them right back in prison.

One particular conversation struck me as a great example to illustrate the concept this chapter is about.

"You don't disrespect somebody," Angel said.

"So you want to be respected?" I asked.

Angel looked confused, but he nodded his head and replied, "Yeah."

Angel was a recovering gang member I worked with while teaching at Homeboy.

I think I understood his confusion. You see, a lot of the gang members are running the mantra "Don't disrespect me." Common sense would suggest that the conversion would be "I want to be respected," but actually that would be a different paradigm.

As mentioned earlier in this book, what you focus on expands, so focusing on what you don't want makes it inevitable that you will get more of what you don't want. Just a simple shift could save countless lives. Gun battles because someone "disrespected" someone else would be over if instead of the dynamic of looking for "disrespect" to combat or avenge, the gang member simply sought out opportunities to be respected.

The truth is that the internal reality—the pattern that has been "running the show" in the heads of these young people—pertains to being shamed. They learned what to do and what not to do by humiliation. Often in examining their childhood, I came to understand that their parents tended to berate them or beat them for the slightest indiscretion. But the beatings tended to be more intense than just a few whacks on the butt; they tended to involve extreme humiliation (abuse).

They are part of a collective or group of people who project and internalize the hurt and pain from their emotional history onto one another.

Domination and Submission

The world these young men and women grew up in involved domination and submission in the home environment, but also in the streets. The reactive world of the inner city is fueled by primal survival instincts. There is a "survival-of-the-fittest" type of mentality, where those who can dominate others seem to have power and control. Fight-or-flight instincts lead some people to act overly aggressive and others to act overly passive.

Growing up, when my homeboys and homegirls left their parents' sphere of influence, they almost always came under control of a gang, often with a more violent set of codes enforced through humiliation. Subsequently, these gang members were "walking the world" focused on whether someone was trying to humiliate them (disrespect) or not.

Obviously, with such a focus (remember *projection and internalizing*), the likelihood that they would encounter humiliation and feel "disrespected" was a virtual certainty.

Not surprisingly, when working with these young men and women, I found that when they were upset, they tended to interpret disrespect coming from somewhere. The defensive posture of other homeboys and homegirls provided a fount of disrespect to project onto. There was always a convenient place to transfer the energy.

> Upset, unchecked, always finds a place to land.

I watched friends nearly come to blows over perceived disrespect. On the occasions that I was present to intervene in these types of conflicts, I found that at least one of the individuals were already struggling with something in their lives that had nothing to do with the person they accused of "disrespecting" them. Most often, both individuals reported having a "bad day" when the conflict arose. I referred to this as *matching energy*. (I'll talk more about this concept later in the book when I discuss managing energy.) Both individuals were upset, and they simply found one another to project their upset onto.

Getting Personal: The Bully on the Block

When I was growing up, there was a kid whose parents were very abusive. He was the angriest human being I had ever met. I befriended him in order to avoid being the object of his anger. I didn't hang out with him much, but every time I saw him, I acted as though I was excited to see him. The truth is that he really scared me and I wanted to get away from him as quickly as I could.

Somehow, he survived childhood and seemingly found a successful career. Not surprisingly, he became a cop. I saw him at my twentieth high school reunion. I spoke with him for only a few minutes and I could tell that nothing had changed; he was still an angry person and I still wanted to get away from him as quickly as possible. I could just imagine him driving around in his cop car looking for "bad guys" on whom to project his anger.

The Cycle Continues

Breaking dysfunctional cycles is hard. In families, communities, and countries where an abusive pattern of dominance and submission has taken root, it is very hard to convince people to end the cycle. We see this with warlords in Somalia, as well as gangs in South Central and East L.A.

In the inner city, the police play a big part in the dysfunction. The gang members are often humiliated by the cops. It is an interesting dynamic. The sad truth is that everyone in the inner city must participate in the reality the cops and gang members have created.

I have found that when some of these young men and women are able to observe their own patterns and come to terms with them, it empowers them to finally leave their limiting environment; of course, returning can then be hazardous to their health. They have broken a key agreement—that anyone who dares to better himself is in some way belittling (or disrespecting) those left behind. Also, the police are not always cooperative in allowing a former gang member to quit the "game." My students report being harassed, and several have been picked up for parole violations, just as they are starting to put their lives together. In L.A., there is a gang injunction that gives the police broad rights to arrest, detain, and charge former gang members. For example, just being within a certain distance of other known gang members is a violation. This basically means that anyone traveling in a particular gang neighborhood can be arrested at any time.

The Shadow in Our Lives

I have spoken about gangs, which tends to be an extreme example of more subtle systems that operate in many families and cultures. If we look deeply into our own lives, we may discover subtle versions of the dominance and submission patterns I have spoken about. Children on the playground often exhibit these behavior patterns. Parents who use punishment and fear to control their children may be unconsciously employing this pattern. Many teachers unknowingly use tactics that perpetuate dominance and submission. On some level, I believe that virtually all people who have grown up in Western culture (and other cultures as well) have experienced this dynamic. We all have some healing to do.

The first step for anyone seeking to heal is to develop the ability to observe the negative patterns that have shaped their reality. And then, the more difficult step (even if it begins to happen naturally) is to drop or *release* the connections that have reinforced the negative patterns. To leave a gang, an abusive family, an unfulfilling job, an uncomfortable living situation, or whatever is not working is a big challenge. It is hard to break agreements and change patterns—because on some level, they are comfortable.

It may be hard for an outsider to see a gang member's circumstances as "comfortable," but for many of the young men and women with whom I work at Homeboy, it is all they've ever known. They have learned to be successful in the eyes of their peers, playing by the rules of their environment. Just getting a full-time job where they have to dress in strange clothes and adapt to an alien set of rules and codes is terrifying.

How Victim Consciousness Perpetuates Itself

I mentioned earlier that the cops and the gang members must all agree to play out the dynamic or it falls apart. There is a part of this dynamic I refer to as *victim consciousness.* In most circumstances, there must be two people willing to play out the victim-and-perpetrator paradigm or the dynamic will no longer occur. There are a lot of angry people who are willing to play the role of perpetrator, but I believe that (in most cases) someone must also be willing to play the role of victim. We see this often in the case of domestic violence, where the "victim" continues to stay with the perpetrator in spite of viable opportunities to leave. The question is, what is the payoff for staying in this type of circumstance?

In the case of domestic violence, the evidence seems clear that the victim is not benefiting from the dynamic, but obviously, there is something unconscious at work in this type of scenario. When we each take a look at our own lives, we may be surprised to find instances where we play the victim. Think about it. Do you catch yourself complaining about situations that could easily be remedied? If so, then you are playing the victim. Now, consider what you get for the position you are taking.

I often say, "There are a lot of victims out there looking for perpetrators." This seems like a dramatic statement, and coming from this Western culture, it is. We tend to like the story we have collectively bought into where someone is always right and someone is always wrong.

Just as taking responsibility is empowering, playing the victim and blaming people or circumstances is disempowering.

Let me be clear: There are absolutely innocent victims who just happen to be in the wrong place at the wrong time. Children are born as innocents, and things that happen to them are not in their control. However, at some point, childhood ends and we must begin to take responsibility for our lives.

Still, generally, we like to believe that there are good guys and bad guys—it empowers our judgment. For example, in our culture, someone to blame is a profitable target for litigation attorneys everywhere. Rooting out the bad guys and the triumph of good over evil is the theme of countless action films released daily by Hollywood studios. We, as a culture, have consumed a story that is not serving us. The belief structure that guides our thinking is fundamentally flawed.

Getting Personal: Getting Out of the Way of Victimhood

I was recently at a sandwich shop ordering lunch, and the order taker was clearly having a bad day. Frankly, her tone was rude and dismissive as she took my order. But I refused to match her energy. I would not engage in her drama. I could just sense that she wanted to cast me as the perpetrator of whatever drama she was playing out. And if I gave her any ammunition—if I gave her any attitude—she would feel justified in dumping all of her negativity on me. Then, presumably, the scene would escalate. If I chose to engage, then I might vent my anger at her, so she could vent more anger at me, with inner justification.

> It is as if many of us carry around the script for the play, a drama that we continually impose on situations. We are casting—like a film director would—people we encounter into the different roles that we need in order to replay the same script again and again. Like moods, emotional scripts cause us to misperceive the world.
> —Paul Ekman

She could push the script all the way to the point where the manager would become involved and possibly fire her. I would then be "the mean man in line who got her fired." This would only serve to fuel more anger and justification (and this would be very similar to the stories I hear at Homeboy).

Fortunately, my inner observer kicked in.

I wanted no part of the drama, so I politely got what I wanted and stepped aside. As I sat down, I observed a person in line fall right into her drama. He confronted her. He complained. He hooked right into her unconscious trap. She identified him as a worthy perpetrator. As I watched, along with the others in line, the drama escalated until—sure enough—a manager came out.

Can you imagine the rest of each of their respective days? Each would likely carry that drama with them like a dark cloud. The customer's lunch would be ruined. The manager would relive the drama countless times as he took whatever disciplinary action he determined was appropriate. The girl would leave work with an arsenal of angry excuses and "mean people" to project her story onto.

Who knows how many people were willing to plug into the negativity after that event? Each of these people would propel their negativity out into the world as the internal toll disturbed their peace. Countless stomachs would end up churning; dozens of people would be wronged.

With just a bit of self-observation and compassion, all of this anger and drama can be avoided. From my perspective, it was all a total waste of energy. I took three clearing breaths and had a nice lunch.

Food and Weight

As you begin to take a look at your story around food and/or weight, consider the position you have taken. As you examine the patterns, beliefs, and agreements, it may serve you to hold the victim/perpetrator concept in your consciousness.

Exercise: Getting in Touch with Your Victim

I would like you to get in touch with the victim in yourself. Write a story from the victim's perspective. I want you to really give the victim a voice, so that you are clear in your life when this aspect of you is coming forward. The more you give yourself to this exercise, the better. Really allow the victim to exaggerate the blame and point the finger at all of the possible perpetrators you can. In the next chapter, we will explore taking responsibility, so keep this story handy. You will be reframing it.

16.
Taking Responsibility

Getting Personal: Fault

"It is not my fault," my teenage stepson Josh would say.

"Whose fault is it?" I would ask.

He was a smart kid, so he could always find a "valid" excuse for why he didn't do well on a test, forgot to turn in his homework, stayed out past his curfew, or whatever came up.

We didn't own a dog, so "the dog ate it" wasn't relevant, but he could come up with a thousand other seemingly legitimate explanations for how he got into whatever predicament he was in. As we went through this parent/teen interaction, I would always come to the part where we investigate what might he have done differently and what choices can he make in the future to avoid this type of situation. This is where the actual learning occurred—for both of us.

Most of the reasons my stepson came up with were concocted and, at best, only represented a fraction of the truth—but he could invest in his story with the best of them. Even if it was an outright lie, he would stay with his excuse like a captain going down with the ship. His ship sank more than once and he would lose some privilege, be given some new restriction, or be assigned some added chore. Ultimately, the opportunity in his failures was to explore the topic of personal responsibility.

I realize that most parents see this ritual as a bother, but it actually has an important purpose. Teaching my son to tell the truth even if it was, "I wanted to play video games and I didn't want to do my homework," was a tremendous gift to him and to me.

Josh provided me a mirror to better see myself. I still concoct my own stories to justify my behavior. I watch myself manipulate circumstances to explain why I react, forget, or don't follow through in situations in my life.

Teaching Josh about integrity forced me to look at my own integrity. Josh was often the first to point out my shortcomings when I was grilling him on his. "Remember when you …" It was hard to say "you're right" to your child when you're playing the role of parent, but it was paramount to being effective with him. Like all kids, he has a built-in "bullshit detector." He had witnessed me being "out of integrity," he noticed it and he remembered—even if I thought he hadn't.

I had to let my stepson know that being in integrity is hard and that I still struggle with it. It seems easier to make up excuses or find someone or something to blame. My integrity is based on my ability to see the whole picture and take responsibility for whatever part I am playing in the given situation.

What I found ultimately was that the fewer excuses either of us made, the more direct and honest our dialogue became—and the more likely each of was to come clean and take personal responsibility for our actions.

I have found that showing my humanity to my kids allows them to see me embrace my own fears and admit that I don't know everything. This allows me to model how each of us must face our own life challenges.

Once Josh and I reshaped our arguments into discussions and adopted a stance of integrity, we had fewer negative feelings about our interactions. A bond of trust began to form that replaced the roles of nagging parent and rebellious teenager.

Taking Responsibility: Embracing the Idea of No Fault

For anyone struggling with weight issues, observation and compassion are important steps on the road to self-acceptance. Now it is time to add the next critical element to the process—responsibility. You need to get rid of the phrase, "it wasn't my fault." The trick is to shift to "no fault" (like the auto insurance that is offered in some states), because it is far more constructive than spending a lot of energy on blame. On the other side of all of the stories you have told and continue to tell is a human experience that makes sense. Taking responsibility for your feelings and your behavior is a major step toward becoming the "you" you were born to be.

Traditional Therapy

Because healing is the process of applying compassion and love to hurt, traditional therapy can be cathartic—but it is not always effective. Where therapy goes wrong is in assigning blame—not empowering people to take responsibility.

Tracking emotional history is fine, but as mentioned earlier in this book, my sense is that it has been given too much attention. In traditional psychotherapy, many people become what I call "therapized"—assigning all negative patterns to past events and interpreting the past from the shame, blame, and guilt paradigm, where someone or something was the cause of their pain.

When people *think* they understand their past, they often use it to absolve themselves of any responsibility. The famed Menendez trial during the 1990s was a great example of this—two adult men killed their wealthy parents and blamed it on an abusive childhood.

The Spiritual Perspective

I believe it is a spiritual perspective that allows for healing and transformation. The higher perspective is that we have all been hurt and we have all hurt others. We are all wounded—maturity is recognizing the hurt but not getting stuck there. This begins with developing the conscious compassionate observer who can perceive patterns without judgment and begin to visualize a different way of being with circumstances that we find challenging.

Accountability vs. Responsibility

Before going any further, however, let me make one fundamental point: The principle of holding individuals, organizations, or companies accountable for their behavior is critical to maintaining healthy relationships as well as creating a just and equitable society. But taking responsibility for our part in the circumstances we face is essential to personal growth and fulfillment. Accountability, when properly applied, should not be intended to blame or scapegoat. Accountability should be rooted in honesty and should always allow the opportunity for making amends.

It is important for society, but it is also vital for conscious individuals to practice taking responsibility. In our childhood, most of us were not rewarded for accountability. We were all too often punished when we admitted mistakes. When most of us were growing up, very few adults asked us to explain why we did what we did; few adults ever truly listened to our explanations or empathized with our position or reasoning. We were simply told that we were bad or wrong when we did something our parents or caregivers didn't like.

When a society does not allow for atonement but rather seeks retribution, the collective shadow will grow, and a cancer of lies and deceit will permeate the culture. With people to blame, a culture will fill countless prisons. Courts become clogged with lawsuits. Outside of the country, as well as within, there will always be an enemy to fight.

Like the society at large, when you are ready to conceive a new vision of the future, it must also encompass an honest recognition that you are responsible for your own reactions. Now, instead of blaming circumstances, you may begin to realize that through honesty and accountability, life becomes more fulfilling. When we dwell in "what is," we begin to recognize that there is a profoundly deep and loving system at work in nature—the natural order of things is basically just. (From a spiritual perspective, there are things like "karma" and "dharma" or divine justice—notions of a "right order," where justice ultimately prevails.)

> Taking responsibility is empowering because you become the author of your own story.

*As **a person with weight-related issues**: When you become adept at taking full responsibility, you will begin to decide how you want to relate to your body, how you want to care for it, and what you want to put into it. Responsibility is related to the notion of "ownership."*

Exercise: Reframing the Victim Experience

Revisit the victim story you wrote as the exercise in the previous chapter. After re-reading it, I want you to reframe it. Take responsibility for the part you play or have played in the dynamic. Imagine with empathy the history or challenges the other party or parties must be fueled by. See all of the learning opportunities for yourself and others in the circumstances.

17.
Acceptance/Surrender

Getting Personal: An Example of Surrender and Acceptance

When my business was "coming apart at the seams" and bankruptcy seemed imminent, I was forced to really learn the principles of surrender and acceptance. I would wake up at four o'clock in the morning, stressing out. I was filled with fear and anxiety. I would rehash past events, feeling a sense of shame at decisions I made that did not turn out the way I expected.

I had a major victim story running nonstop in my head. I saw all of the players in my personal drama who had wronged me. I felt inclined to justify my feelings by blaming others.

But when I *surrendered* to the circumstances, things began to lift. I opened up to an attitude of learning and growth. I looked at all of the participants in a different way. I saw them as my teachers. I saw the situation as an opportunity to practice *acceptance*. My shift allowed me to receive a flow of positive energy based on *reframing* the situation from a learning perspective. (We'll discuss "Learning Perspective" more in the next chapter.)

I saw that being a real estate developer was not my life's purpose, just a stop along the way. I became so grateful for the lessons that real estate development taught me. When I began to step into the pain, it began to shift. My mantra became "with compassion and humility, I embrace my experience as the launching pad for the life I was born to lead."

When you experience something painful, you have two choices: judge the pain as "bad" and resist it, or accept it and open up to what it might have to teach you. Resistance to pain makes it stronger, because resistance is a form of denial of "what is"—which is not just futile but tends to make matters worse.

Surrendering to "What Is": The Undertow

The undertow at the beach is a wonderful metaphor for the need to *surrender* and to allow the current of life to take you under. If you don't panic, you will pop right back up again. The master surfer rides the wave, and if he wipes out, he surrenders to the tide and it gently carries him back to safety. The surfer knows better than to struggle against the water's flow. He realizes that the ocean is larger and more powerful than him.

However, if you fight it, you will surely have a much harder time, and it is even possible that the undertow might pull you under and you will drown. The panic of being out of control and not knowing how long and how far down the current may pull a person can bring about their death.

As a person with weight-related issues: *You will release weight as the need to find comfort for your pain drops away. You can embrace your challenges and be naturally pulled into a new version of "you."*

Staying Unattached

The unconscious part of us, programmed with beliefs about how things "ought to be," is attached to the outcome. We tend to react automatically when things seemingly don't go our way. As our observer develops, we can track our reactions and consciously intercept our perceptions. We can choose how we want to view circumstances and how we would like to respond to situations as they occur.

Remember, our higher intention is often polluted by the residual effect of years of programming by our tribe to over-identify with the material world. Staying "unattached to the outcome" takes diligence and practice—we are continually challenged to go deeper.

Accepting All that Is
(and Viewing All Circumstances as Perfect)

Many experiences in life are difficult, even painful, but that does not make them mistakes. There is a principle in many teachings that God does not make mistakes. The first principle of personal fulfillment is that everything is perfect. Every circumstance, every event, every experience in your life is perfect, because it is a product of the natural order of things, of which you and your judgment are but a minuscule part.

> What has happened was supposed to happen—the evidence is: because it did.

My professor, Dr. Ron Hulnick, in the spiritual psychology program at the University of Santa Monica said, **"Pain is part**

of life, but suffering is optional." He went on to explain how the interpretation that an event or circumstance should not have happened was what causes suffering.

Painful experiences can be opportunities for learning if we are open and accepting of the lessons that they have to teach us. The spiritual principle of mystery, in ancient times practiced in so-called mystery schools, holds that no human knows exactly what is going to happen to him or her, nor why things are playing out the way that they are, so any investment in "ought to" and "should have" will invariably lead to torment. The higher perspective is that everything happens for a reason, and when viewed accurately, there are always opportunities for growth.

> Stepping into the Mystery means surrendering to the forces that swirl around us. Such a surrender, far from a defeat, is a way for us to grow larger and more connected. – John Lee

Exercise: Accept Your Body

Find a time and place where you will not be disturbed for at least thirty minutes. Close your eyes, and use your hands to explore your body—all over. Have a verbal dialogue with your body. Let it know that you have judged it, neglected it, and abused it—but now you are committing to accepting and loving it. Try to stay with this process for at least ten minutes—even if you repeat yourself over and over again.

People often experience deep feelings around sexual or emotional centers (referred to in Eastern spiritual traditions as chakras), located in the stomach, pelvic, and groin areas of their bodies. As these feelings come up, don't resist them—surrender and accept them. Be as kind and nurturing to yourself as possible.

When you open your eyes, I want you to write in your journal about your relationship with your body. It may be valuable to track how you have related to your body in the past. You may find it healing to "give your body a voice" and allow it to inform you about the experience your body has had. Before you complete the exercise, commit in writing to accepting and loving your body.

I believe that your body is your teacher—it holds the key to unlocking the power of your human experience. In the deep relationship with your humanity, you will find your "gold"— that profound connection to your divine essence and unique human experience.

Abuse and a Profound Disconnection from the Body

If you have experienced abuse in your life, you may have found the last exercise very hard to do—if not impossible. I mentioned earlier in the book about carrying extra weight as protection—which can be common if someone has been physically or sexually abused.

Part of the protection mechanism tends to be a disconnection from the body. The individual who has experienced abuse—often at the hands of a parent or close family member—must literally disconnect from his or her body to survive. I have heard adults, in processing childhood abuse, describe an experience of lifting out of their body while the abuse was occurring.

The challenge for many of the people who have experienced abuse is to get back into their bodies. On some level in their psyche, the individuals do not feel safe "in their body." So asking someone who has cut off from his or her body to have a dialogue with that body can be more than challenging.

This book, unfortunately, won't provide specific enough exercises for someone struggling with this particular dynamic. What this book can offer, however, is a general roadmap that can be supplemented with other healing modalities.

Everyone reading this book will have some component of his or her personal process that this book simply doesn't cover thoroughly enough. Part of developing a "self-care practice," which you will do later in this book, is to find activities or processes to enhance this "general roadmap." This is why early in the book I suggest doing some type of body work as a supplement.

Trauma

I feel compelled to discuss trauma a little further. The psychiatric community generally has held the opinion that intense trauma cannot be fully healed. They often see long-term anti-depressant care (drugs like Prozac) combined with traditional talk therapy as the way to maintain some control over the effects of trauma, but they don't see a clear avenue to healing.

I believe trauma can be healed, and I have witnessed traumatized people heal. The challenge is that there is no single process that works for everyone. I have seen positive results from "somatic" body work. Dr. Peter Levine, the founder of Somatic Experiencing, is an excellent resource for exploring this type of work. (See appendix for more information.)

18.
A Learning Perspective

Getting Personal: Learning and Growing

As mentioned in the previous chapter, we often learn by making what are perceived to be mistakes, but I view them as learning opportunities.

When my two-year-old daughter Isabella began climbing on the back of an oversized chair in the living room, my wife and I immediately told her to get down. But because she was two, she climbed up again and again. We warned her that she might fall, and eventually she did.

I was filled with guilt as we drove Isabella to the emergency room to have the gash in her chin sewn up. It happened on "my watch." In the car, my wife asked me what happened, and I informed her that I had just told Isabella to get down and pulled her off of the chair a few minutes before she fell. Clearly, Isabella had waited until I was occupied with something else, and she climbed up when I wasn't looking.

For the story's sake, I would like to say that Isabella never climbed on the chair again, but the truth is that she still scales the oversized chair and many other "peaks" of furniture in our house. But she seems to be more careful. And when she recognizes that she is in a precarious position where she might fall, she will now often come off the ledge herself or call for help. Knowing my daughter, it may take quite a few more falls before she masters the heights she seems destined to climb.

How We View Failure

Clearly, falling is a natural part of the process of learning how to climb, just as failure is inherent in learning. So if you are going to climb, if you are going to challenge yourself to expand beyond your present circumstances, you will ultimately be faced with setbacks. However, if you view the setbacks as temporary and you truly grasp the important learning opportunity in the experience, you will ultimately reach new heights.

And when you get there, you will have something special to savor, because you will know what it took to rise above your fear and challenge yourself to go for what you want. More importantly, you will have developed a sense of confidence in your ability to overcome hurdles and challenges, and a sense of your own strength and resourcefulness.

> We would never think to blame an infant for falling down when he or she is beginning to walk, because we understand that falling is part of the process of learning to walk.

Nurture a Learning Perspective toward Life

When judgment about oneself and attachment to outcome are replaced by devotion to the process of growth, every problem can be *reframed* as an opportunity. For those of us who struggle with weight this means seeing the deeper truth about our relationship with food and with our bodies.

When you have a learning perspective toward life, you begin to realize that success and failure are a bad bargain because they are judgments, and judgment stands in the way of authenticity and intimacy. No one has ever shamed or guilt tripped themselves into loving themselves (this is why diets don't work).

We cannot really know ourselves or others if we are caught up in judgment. By its very nature, judgment is inaccurate—because everything you judge, when viewed with compassion and understanding, begins to make sense.

Of course, the person we have been trained to judge the most is ourselves, and the actions that we scrutinize most closely are our own. But you can only grow and release weight by having compassion for yourself. Every event, every feeling, every experience can become a learning opportunity when you view it from an open, compassionate perspective. When you see life as a great learning adventure, the future seems to open up and appears far less ominous and scary.

Exercise: My Biggest Lesson

I want you to take this opportunity to reframe a past experience from a learning perspective. This is your chance to retell a story that you have told (perhaps countless times) in a new way that allows you to move the situation out of the realm of disappointment or mistake and into a new reality of growth and "upliftment."

19.

Making an Internal Shift

Getting Personal: Seeing a "Problem" Differently

I was in a car accident recently. After making sure no one was hurt, I caught my mind racing into the future and coming up with negative scenarios (negative fantasy of the future) such as: the rest of the day is ruined; now I'll have to call my insurance (my rates will probably go up); I have to go to a body shop, rent a car, reschedule appointments, and on and on.

Instead of allowing myself to "go there," with some deep breaths and by checking in, I was able to shift my perspective. I decided to view the experience differently—I was fortunate that it wasn't worse; my day had simply changed. I wondered how it would turn out and what I would learn from the experience.

In exchanging information, I realized that the other party was insured and reasonable. My interaction with the other person was courteous and pleasant. The body shop had a relationship with the car rental company that made the process fairly easy. And I got to drive a car I really liked for a week while my vehicle was repaired. I met a nice attendant at the car rental agency, who recommended a wonderful bistro for lunch, where I later took my wife on "date night."

Choose How You Want to Experience Life

In this instance, I realized that a lot of good things developed because I maintained an open mind and didn't struggle with my new circumstances.

Things have a remarkable way of working out when we learn to surrender to the natural flow of life. In any given moment, where we can shift out of negativity and stay open to the experience, life tends to bless us with positive occurrences. This is primarily an inside job—we must learn to cultivate an inner authority that can step in and reframe situations, helping us avoid falling into negativity and the chain of unconstructive reactions that follow negative energy.

Exercise: Shift Your Energy and Watch Your Life Unfold

In this exercise, we are building on the concept of *choice*. Similar to a learning perspective toward life, viewing things differently can have a powerful impact on your day-to-day experience. Parallel to reframing the past, seeing things differently allows you to make choices about how you want to view circumstances as they actually occur.

In your journal, I want you to write the title "seeing things differently." Set an intention to shift your perspective, and write the intention down. Give yourself ten journal pages to revisit when a challenging circumstance comes up. In the next day or two, try to find an event where you can practice this skill.

Write in your journal about the event; be sure to include how you might have responded in the past. Explore how circumstances may have played out differently as well, if you had reacted with negativity and judgment.

20.

Beyond Judgment and into Meaning

Getting Personal: Pushed to Grow

I grew up with a close family friend who was only a few weeks older than I. The two of us were remarkably similar in many ways. However, there was one major difference between us that I believe made a tremendous difference in our lives. My friend's family had a lot of money. My family didn't have a lot of money.

For most of my life, I believed his wealth was an advantage, but I see now what a disadvantage it really was and how useful my own experience has proven to be.

Because my parents didn't have extra money to give me, and as a teenager I needed spending money to maintain a social life, I began taking jobs as soon as I was legally allowed to work. Before I graduated from high school, I had already worked at McDonald's, an ice-cream shop, the shipping department of a computer software company, a phone bank for a marketing research firm, a contractor, and a landscaper. Because of my work experience, I learned different skills and overcame many fears.

By the time my friend graduated high school, he had never had a job outside of the family business. Until his premature death at thirty-three, he seemed to wander through the world trying to discover what he should be doing in life. But because he had a trust fund and was financially independent, he spent most of his time lost in confusion. He took a lot of vacations (which I envied at the time) and had a lot of hobbies and interests, but no real purpose.

I learned purpose and meaning by experiencing life in seemingly mundane ways. I discovered so much about myself because of necessity. I was pushed by life into many different circumstances that I might never have chosen if I didn't need a job—and all of them had something to teach me. One example is the phone bank; at first I hated cold calling and interviewing people, but I learned to get good at it. Eventually the company I worked for even sent me out on field assignments to conduct surveys. My ability to approach people and the confidence I gained in my communications skills have been tremendously helpful in my life.

Each work experience led to some new adventures that forged an "education in real life." These adventures and life skills gave me the confidence and resourcefulness to adapt as life threw curves at me, and eventually to attract the teachings that became this book. At every turn, my desire to explore and grow provided a direction and gave my life meaning.

The Importance of Meaning
"Meaning" is a philosophical question, but a rather important one—frequently overlooked in our fast-moving culture—"what

gives life meaning?" And "what meaning can we derive from life's experiences?"

From a fact-oriented, scientific perspective, meaning is often considered irrelevant. Too often, questions about "the meaning of life" get confused looks, or those who ask the question are chided for "wasting time pondering abstract philosophy."

To quote Dr. Rachel Naomi Remen, one of the earliest pioneers in the mind/body holistic health movement, "meaning helps us to see in the dark." Meaning turns a difficult experience from a curse into a blessing.

Meaning, in other words, is the foundation of *reframing* and can become the basis for a key skill required in transformation—finding meaning.

For example, the medical profession tends to ignore the meaning of illness. However, traditional Chinese medicine suggests that illness occurs when a person is "out of balance." A traditional Chinese doctor will seek to help the patient get back in energetic balance as a means of curing the disease. The meaning of the illness is fundamental to the choices of care provided.

Thus, illness has the potential to draw our attention to imbalance in our lives. From a spiritual perspective, illness exists to teach us something about being human. Meaning is derived from profound experiences, such as illness, and it is meaning that makes our lives significant. I believe that we get sick because we are out of alignment with our authenticity—when we go against our true inner nature to please others or comply with expectations.

For those of us who struggle with weight, there is important meaning in the challenges we face. We must develop a reverence and respect for our individual human journey toward wholeness. Once again, this can only begin to occur when we have released judgment.

Viktor Frankl

One of the most famous books about meaning is Viktor Frankl's work, *Man's Search for Meaning,* which formed the basis of a branch of psychology he called Logotherapy. Frankl, a psychiatrist in Austria, was imprisoned by the Nazis during World War II, and attributed his survival to his inner observer—the ability to not identify with his horrific circumstances but instead to see everything that was occurring as part of a greater reality.

Frankl was a man of great inner strength and will, and he was able to maintain an inner sense of freedom in the face of incredible cruelty, which allowed him to live moment to moment and find meaning in every second of life. He didn't hold on too tightly to any specific interpretation, but allowed meaning to unfold organically. This type of fluid relationship with life experiences is a fundamental part of the Service to Self™ process.

Frankl put it this way:

> [T]he meaning of life differs from man to man, from day to day and from hour to hour. What matters, therefore, is not the meaning of life in general but rather the specific meaning of a person's life at a given moment. To put the

question in general terms would be comparable to the question posed to a chess champion: "Tell me, Master, what is the best move in the world?" There simply is no such thing as the best or even a good move apart from a particular situation in a game and the particular personality of one's opponent. The same holds for human existence. One should not search for an abstract meaning of life. Everyone has his own specific vocation or mission in life to carry out a concrete assignment which demands fulfillment. Therein he cannot be replaced, nor can his life be repeated. Thus, everyone's task is as unique as is his specific opportunity to implement it.[*]

Frankl suggests that meaning is dynamic, always changing, and subject to each particular individual and circumstance. For him, the focus is not necessarily on some overarching meaning to life—rather, meaning occurs for an individual in each moment of that person's life.

Meaning as Fulfillment

There is an opportunity to shape our lives based on a developed conscious orientation toward finding meaning. I believe that my friend's circumstances from the story at the start of this chapter may have deprived him of an essential spiritual imperative—finding meaning in life based on experience. Interestingly, I spent time with him as he was dying from cancer, and we had really

[*]   *Man's Search for Meaning* by Viktor E. Frankl Copyright © 1959, **1962, 1984, 1992 by Viktor E. Frankl. Reprinted by permission of Beacon Press, Boston**

deep, meaningful conversations. It was as if his illness made his relationships and the challenges he had faced in his life more meaningful. I often wonder how his life might have been different had he survived.

It is important to note that Maslow's hierarchy of human needs culminates in self-actualization, which might easily be considered a synonym for finding meaning.

The key thing to remember here is that by making conscious choices, we reinforce and create meaning in all of the areas of our lives, and by honoring ourselves with compassion and forgiveness, we strengthen our ability to continue to make positive, life-affirming decisions, which gives our life meaning.

Finally, when we embrace this way of being, we cannot support a negative choice that harms us—and all aspects of a destructive behavior pattern must ultimately drop away. First the negative patterns become our teacher, so that we can overcome our misunderstandings. Then, when our consciousness connects us to a deeper meaning and purpose for our lives, we adjust our patterns to truly meet our needs and propel us toward fulfillment—we release weight because we eat well and take care of our bodies as part of our purpose.

Exercise: Meaning

This exercise can be done in several different ways. I purposefully want to leave it open so that you can discover whatever meaning you need to connect with at this moment.

The first way to approach this exercise is to find an event that you have already assigned a particular meaning to, and re-interpret the meaning. In other words, explore an interpretation you have about a past event—look for stories that you have been telling about something dramatic or traumatic in your life, and assign a new meaning to that event.

The other approach is to take an event that you have been confused about and explore its meaning from a higher perspective. Find meaning in that event that serves you. Don't be concerned if you are "making it up"—the truth is that any meaning that we derive from circumstances or events in our lives is "made up." **Meaning lies in us,** not in the actual event.

Write about meaning in your journal—leaving some pages open to revisit the section later, as you discover new meanings. When you are open to meaning, you will find meaning—often in seemingly meaningless events.

21.
Leading with Your Strengths

Getting Personal: Let the Good Times Roll

Often in my past, when I felt like I was on a roll and things were going well, I had a looming notion that the positive wave would eventually crash into the rocks. My good fortune would end. The good times wouldn't last. I simply wasn't confident enough in myself to believe I deserved whatever good fortune was coming my way.

I remember when my current wife and I were dating, I kept warning her that I wasn't really as great a guy as I seemed to be. I didn't want her to be disappointed when she witnessed what I judged to be my negative traits. Slowly, bit by bit, as I revealed what I deemed to be flaws, I became more comfortable with the idea that she might just love the whole me. The challenge, of course, was for **me** to learn to love the whole me.

I spent many years being cautious—restricted by my negative self-image. I was very concerned with what other people thought of me. However, I have methodically adjusted my life to focus on my strengths and surround myself with supportive people and situations that allow me to shine. I am committed to leading with my strengths. This concept has not always been easy to embrace, but with conscious practice, it has grown to be my primary "mode of operation"—*I lead with my strengths and my positive intent—let the chips fall where they may.*

Practice Giving the Gift of Your Talents and Abilities

What would it look like to orient your life so that you are giving a gift to the world by offering your unique talents and abilities in service to the greater good? This concept may seem odd at first, but I believe that each of us has a unique opportunity to enrich the world by becoming the person we were born to be.

As your personal process continues to develop, consider the vulnerability that you may have viewed as a weakness becoming a source of empowerment. Your individual challenges with food and weight may shift from a tragic story to a personal triumph, and the spirit of the human being behind your authentic experience may be a gift that you have to give others.

It may take some practice, but I believe it is not just our birthright but our responsibility to embrace our experiences and become self-actualized.

Exercise: Inventory of Strengths—Letting Your Light Shine

I want you to take this opportunity to list your gifts, talents, and abilities.

In the next week, I want you to find opportunities to shine. In other words, risk being good at something—this could be truly minor. If you're a good cook, then bake something special and share it at work— perhaps take on some responsibility you know you can excel at. Just find a way to "come out" a little and "let your light shine."

I want you to write in your journal about the experience.

22.
Creating a Vision and Watching Miracles Unfold

Old Abe and the Flood

Down around Louisiana, folks tell a story about an old-timer named Abe. Everyone always said that Abe was a man of incredible faith. Abe lived in a small single-story shack. He was a simple, churchgoing man who never really cared much about material things. He was always doing things for others.

When Hurricane Katrina hit, Abe didn't panic. As the flood waters reached his porch, Old Abe climbed up to the roof. Abe had been a good man all his life, and he just knew that God would spare him from the flood.

As he sat there on the roof, the flood waters rising, a neighbor came by in a rowboat, offering to take him to higher ground. But Abe told him, "No thank you; you go help someone else. I have faith that the Lord with protect and care for me."

A short time later, the flood waters rising faster and faster, a rescue boat arrived and ordered Old Abe to evacuate. But Old

Abe stood his ground, saying strongly, "That won't be necessary. I know God has his hand on my shoulder, and he would never let anything bad happen to me. You go rescue someone else." After a short standoff, the rescue boat left to indeed assist other citizens, and Old Abe stood on his roof watching the flood waters rise.

A few hours later, when the flood waters had reached the eaves of his roof, a National Guard helicopter showed up and lowered a basket to take Old Abe to safety. But Abe pushed it away, waving his hand and shouting, "No thank you, the Lord will provide."

A short time later, after the helicopter had left, with no rescue boat or neighbor to save the old man, Abe drowned.

Now, when Old Abe entered the gates of heaven, he marched straight up to God and proclaimed, "I had such faith in you, Lord. How could you have let me drowned like that?"

To which God replied, "What are you talking about? I sent a rowboat, a power rescue boat, and even a helicopter."

The Nature of Miracles

This story is most often told as an anecdote regarding blind faith, and it can easily be viewed as such. But I believe the story has a stronger message. Having done the vision work I am about to describe in this chapter, and having used it with a number of clients, I have witnessed miraculous transformations. I have seen countless prayers answered as people's circumstances dramatically shift. However, it is the nature of the individual's focus that tends to determine the results, and the outcome is very rarely what the person utilizing this tool might have originally imagined. In the story, Abe got his miracle—he just didn't recognize it.

We all have ideas of what a miracle looks like. There are cultural myths of hard-fought success, of setbacks and redemption. I can't remember which actor was living in his car before he was discovered and became a big star—but our culture loves that kind of miracle story. Lottery winners go from rags to riches, and in TV interviews they proclaim that it was their faith that got them through the hard times. Stories we have heard in church or the miracle endings of countless movies and TV programs where the good guy wins seduce us into believing in a fantasy. Now, I am not saying that miraculous things don't happen—I believe they happen all the time, every day. But what I am challenging is the notion that miracles must be dramatic or look a particular way.

Just like in the story of Old Abe, I think that there are opportunities that we let slip by because we are invested in a particular outcome. When we focus on a quality of experience, we find opportunities in perhaps the simplest, most mundane circumstances. This is the true meaning of manifesting—the idea is that you are quite literally creating the experience you want to have. When we tap into our inner authority and begin to recognize the gifts that lay before us, miracles begin to happen.

Getting Personal: My Relationship Vision

During a twelve-week Imago Relationship Workshop held at and sponsored by All Saints Episcopal Church in Pasadena, my wife and I created our relationship vision. For the duration of the class and for several months after the class, my wife and I read the following vision out loud to one another every evening before bed:

Relationship Vision for Freeman & Jasmine

- We feel deeply connected and safe.
- We play and have fun together.
- We relate openly and honestly without fear of saying the "wrong" thing.
- We are grateful for where we live.
- Our faith centers around a knowing that everything is as it should be. Love is the answer to every perceived problem.
- We have a very fulfilling, nurturing, and intimate sex life.
- We love to laugh and go on adventures.
- Our free time is split between being of service and enjoying our family.
- We support each other when we struggle and when we succeed.
- We relate to money with an underlying sense of abundance and without fear.
- We have three wonderful children who are all very close to one another.
- Our children are open and honest with us and we are open and honest with them.
- We are very connected to mutual friends, yet we always hold our partner in our consciousness when relating to the opposite sex.
- We make decisions as a team, and hold the other in our consciousness when having to make decisions when the other partner is not around.
- Conflict is resolved with respect for the other being "other."
- The relationship with our in-laws continues to improve as we work to see their loving essence, and release our judgments about them.

- **We exercise together and separately, and we work as a team to maintain a healthy lifestyle.**
- **We integrate nature into our lives.**
- **We are affectionate with one another.**
- **We enjoy socializing with others, but we work to balance socializing with intimate family time.**
- **We support our children being exactly who they are, and we respect their choices, allowing them the dignity of their own process.**

I can honestly say that my wife and I are living the vision—sometimes, when times get tough, we pull out our vision and read it again, but in general, we have and continue to create the relationship of our dreams—by our conscious choice. We have total faith in our ability to co-create the circumstances to meet each of the items on our list (or replace it with new criteria that we find more fulfilling).

Prior to meeting my wife, I had spent many hours, days, even years, dreaming about "Ms. Right." I searched long and hard to find her—all the while hoping for a miracle—that it was "in my cards" to meet my dream girl, my soul mate, and live happily ever after. When I met my current wife, some part of me had apprehension—the fact that she had a ten-year-old son didn't meet my imagined ideal. Still another part of me was willing to invest in the potential, with some deep faith that she might be "the one."

What I understand now is that the miraculous dwells in our ability to see miracles and co-create with God a life of fulfillment. If we can stay open, yet focused, and keep our attention on the quality of experience we are looking for, we can all have our dreams come true.

For me, the miracle of my life has been the manifesting of my soul mate.

Create Your Vision

By now, we've discussed seeing and doing things differently. In this chapter, we will integrate the third part of this transformative process—imagining things differently. Our imaginations are powerful tools that we often unconsciously use to sabotage ourselves. We project negative future fantasies ahead of our lives and find ourselves playing out these negative impressions of our particular reality. This is often referred to as a self-fulfilling prophecy.

Just as a negative outlook can adversely affect our lives, a positive projected outlook can greatly improve our lives. As you visualize a different future, you are using your imagination to explore the possibilities, to open up to the potential of your life.

Again, I won't go into specifics, but science has begun to recognize the power of thought on the potentiality of certain things occurring. Quantum physicists have begun to acknowledge that a person's perception somehow directly affects the thing a person is viewing. This hasn't been a comfortable notion for many conventional scientists, but it is being borne out by research and experiments in the laboratory.

The Service to Self™ process helps you take the principle of "positive projected potential" and apply it to your life by creating a vision. As you work to interrupt and reframe conditioned beliefs and patterns of behavior, chances are strong that you will begin to imagine new possibilities for your life. You'll want to harness those images to direct and support a vision of your new life.

This is literally giving birth to a new version of you—I've had many clients and colleagues describe the experience using the analogy of sleep. It is as if they had been asleep and suddenly woke up and began feeling "very different" from the *inside*. When they remember their lives prior to doing this work, they report it seeming like a bad dream, but their present reality feels far more real to them.

Exercise: Creating a Life Vision

In this process, you will take the intention tool one step further. You're going use your journal to clearly establish and solidify the future you **intend** to experience.

Center yourself by closing your eyes, and breathe deeply several times. Ask for assistance from your inner authority. Allow your breath to take you on a journey. Imagine your life in five years, with all of your qualities translated into authentic expression of your gifts and talents. Open your eyes, and in your journal, begin writing your vision.

Write out your vision: Start by writing the title: My Life in Five Years. Then under that, write *I am* ... (e.g., "I am living in a nurturing environment, surrounded by nature. I am supporting myself by doing a job that I love. Food has become a wonderful gift in my life. I am honestly and openly ..."). Remember to examine and "source" your vision from the inside out. Try to stay away from external measurements (e.g., I weigh X pounds, or I am making X dollars per month). The vision should be at least 50 percent believable, but don't be scared to stretch.

Try to continue to cultivate the *quality of life* you want as it relates to your deserving positive results and abundance. If you find yourself getting stuck, call on your inner supporter to help you.

Instead of saying you want a specific car, focus instead on the specific qualities of that car that interest you, such as "I want a quality vehicle, a vehicle I can trust." Or "I want a relationship built on trust and honesty. I want people around me with whom I feel comfortable being myself." These are far more important than just material items or ideas of what you want; these are the things that are really going to feed you.

The most important distinction between going for the "quality of experience" rather than imagining an external or material outcome is that you can begin experiencing the quality immediately. You don't need to wait until the material object appears in your life.

So often, what we are looking for is right in front of us, but we cannot see it. I have had clients make minor adjustments in their lives, focusing on the quality of experience they are seeking, and have major shifts in their level of fulfillment by seeing things they already have "for the first time."

Take the life vision in whatever direction it wants to go. Don't judge yourself—whatever you come up with is fine. We are going to work on this more, so you don't need to get this right, because this is just a jumping-off point.

When you are finished, write on the bottom of the last page, "I surrender my limited vision to a greater intelligence for the highest good of all."

Changing the way you look at things makes the things you look at change.

23.

Stepping into Change

Getting Personal: Taking Things One Step at a Time

I don't think anyone ever considered me a patient child—in fact, I would say *impatient* would tend to be the common characterization of me in my youth. As a kid, I always wanted to know "Are we there yet?" So allowing the unfolding of events or taking something one step at a time has always been a challenging proposition for me. As a school-aged boy, several model airplanes sat partially finished in my bedroom, due to the fact that I began gluing parts together before reading the instructions, only to find out that not following the steps in order meant that the plane could no longer be assembled properly.

Over the years, I have come to recognize the wisdom in the old saying "inch by inch it's a cinch, but yard by yard it's hard." But recognizing the wisdom and implementing the principle are two different things. My understanding that some things take time and require a series of small, incremental steps has often been at odds with my desire for instant gratification.

Thus, a good deal of my personal-growth work has centered on accepting and loving the part of me that doesn't want to "take it slow." My personal "inner dialogue" has been a negotiation with the part of me that wants to "be there already." The Service to Self™ process, because I develop it, allows for impatience. In your journal, I encourage you to give this part of you a voice.

Why Step by Step Matters:
Understand that taking things step by step makes change easier to accomplish, and undoubtedly there is something about approaching change incrementally that honors where you are at every interval.

It just seems appropriate to step into any life-changing process slowly. The inclination when one does not like oneself in the present is to demand an instant transformation. For those of us who have struggled with weight, miracle diets, simple procedures, magic pills, wonder straps—all guaranteed to "melt away pounds effortlessly"—have been attractive propositions, even though some part of us knows they won't work. Every year, people throw away millions, if not billions, of dollars on fad diets, ineffective procedures, or mysterious supplements that do nothing but rob them of hope and money. That is not what this process is about. This is a slow process that has the potential to lead to lasting change.

You should be absorbing these ideas gradually and letting them sink in over time. Just as one shouldn't rush off to get married after only knowing a person for a brief period, it is important to establish a relationship with your process that has the potential to last forever.

The Service to Self™ process involves a series of minor adjustments. Your life will change dramatically if you can just take a series of small but intentional and effective steps that support a vision you are holding in your consciousness.

Meeting Your Needs Consciously

We have already established that eating patterns and behavior around food have been attempts to get needs met. But there are other patterns and behavior that don't necessarily involve eating but that pertain to needs.

Codependency

The term *codependent* has been made popular by twelve-step programs (e.g., Alcoholics Anonymous). The term very simply relates to a tendency to create unhealthy patterns in relationships with others. In short, we rely on other people playing particular roles for us to continue a pattern of behavior. Each person is said to be codependent on the other in order to maintain the unhealthy dynamic.

To be quite frank, we have been talking about codependency throughout this book, without necessarily using that label. Earlier in the book, when we discussed unhealthy agreements, we were talking about codependency. A few chapters ago, in our discussion of the victim-and-perpetrator paradigm, we were talking about codependency. In general, I avoid the term because it has become too cliché. I hear it thrown around in casual conversation, and I find it has lost much of its true meaning.

At this point in the book, I bring this term up for two reasons: First because you will hear it out in the world, and it is important to recognize how it might relate to the Service to Self™ process. The second reason pertains to relationships. We often get our needs met in relationships—from intimate relationships to friendships to work relationships. It is important to become conscious about the agreements you are making with those whom you have relationships with. You will want to engage in mutually beneficial relationships that are empowering and uplifting. You will want to avoid codependent relationships where each person is unconsciously using the other person to try to get needs met.

Clear, Healthy Choices to Get Needs Met

The need for intimacy and touch was addressed by a male client of mine who was single and taking a break from dating by having a therapeutic massage once a week. He specifically found a very nurturing woman whose touch felt healing to meet his needs in a safe and healthy way. This was a clear and calculated agreement that met his needs "cleanly." He didn't try to date the massage therapist. He didn't want to hang out with her on weekends or be her friend. He simply hired her to perform a service that helped him meet a specific need. She was pleased to have a pleasant, good-paying, regular customer—that's it.

Another client felt like he needed attention—he had previously beaten himself up for "showing off" or "talking too much" in inappropriate settings. The healthy outlet he discovered was joining a Toastmasters group. Toastmasters is an organization that has chapters across the United States that usually meet once a week; the members all have the chance to get up and practice speaking in front of the group. He simply loved it—he got to "show off" and "talk too much" in a healthy, self-honoring environment. If you don't presently have constructive ways to meet your needs, don't worry about it. That's where we're going next.

Now it is time to build on the work you have already done. You have formed an intention and you are creating a vision for your future. You have been observing and creating an inventory of your unhealthy patterns, agreements, and beliefs. You have a new relationship with your needs. In short, you are nurturing a new sense of yourself.

This newly formed identity is based upon your self-knowledge, including an inventory of your strengths and abilities, as well as a greater understanding of your conditioned reactions and misperceptions. The strategy to meet your needs consciously, which you will be implementing, will support the development and growth of your inner authority. With your inner authority guiding your life, the conscious choices you make will lead toward fulfillment.

Exercise: Practice Meeting Needs

The first exercise you did in this book was an inventory of your needs. Perhaps you have revisited this exercise—if you haven't, we are going back there right now. Pick *one* need that you feel does not get sufficiently met in your current life circumstances. Develop a plan to meet the need consciously, similar to the examples I mentioned above (the massage and Toastmasters). Find at least one opportunity in the next week to explore your choice—write in your journal about your experience.

24.
Successful Strategy

Getting Personal: Manipulation

I used to interpret the word *manipulation* as having a negative connotation. It seemed slippery and dishonest. I never wanted to be accused of manipulating people or circumstances to meet my needs. So I was especially defensive when my ex-wife accused me of being a manipulator in a couples therapy session, while we were still married. I remember the female therapist—whom I had always judged as taking my then wife's side—turning to her and saying "of course he's manipulating; so are you—so is everyone." She went on to explain that manipulating is a way of leveraging and strategizing in order to get needs met. She called on the two of us to consider all of the ways that we might be able to consciously manipulate our resources and circumstances to save our marriage.

Ultimately, no amount of conscious manipulating was able to spare us the pain of divorce. But ever since that moment, I have viewed manipulation from a different perspective. For me, conscious manipulation is just another way of saying: "Have a strategy that utilizes all of your resources in order to get what you want and need."

Creating a Supportive Environment

It is hard to change your life when nothing around you changes. For instance, if you commit to releasing weight but your partner or spouse continues to buy Ding Dongs and eat them in front of you, it may be hard to maintain focus and stay out of old patterns.

Men in particular can sometimes have a tough time admitting they need help—e.g., the time-worn example of their difficulty asking for directions when lost. When doing the Service to Self™ process, you need *support*. That's why using a partner in the exercises and finding encouraging colleagues is so important.

On an emotional, mental, and spiritual level, if you commit to nurturing an experience of a new authentic self but you hang out with the exact same people and engage in exactly the same conversations and behaviors, the chances of your life moving in a different direction are slim. This doesn't mean that you must get a new partner or spouse, or stop relating to your family and friends, but it does mean that you must relate to them differently.

Consider some of the agreements that might presently be affecting your experience. Perhaps your work associates have agreed that "the company sucks." This breeds a negative attitude that will not serve your decision to grow—you'll remain mired in negativity at work (where I imagine you spend a good amount of your time). When you decide to grow and embrace positive change, it may require breaking out of a role or pattern that was part of the dynamic that defined the people or groups you have been associating with.

You will also need allies in this journey. The people presently around you may or may not be serving your aspirations and goals. Try to be perceptive about who is supporting and who is undermining your attempts at becoming a better you.

It is common for people to shift relationships during periods of growth, painful as it may be. This doesn't mean you must drop all friendships you presently have—though, in truth, as you change, some relationships may fall away and be released.

Additionally, you may choose to bow out of certain activities or simply not engage in certain conversations that you determine no longer serve you.

You may be well served by inviting new people into your life. You can choose to hang around people with similar interests who *support* your growth.

Groups, by nature, can be restrictive. The dynamics of a group can keep you from being who you truly are. There may be several factors at play; one is simply that you may feel as though you need the group's acceptance. Many rituals are built around fear of something new and unknown—predictability can be comfortable. Simply offering a new option, a different activity, or engaging in a different type of conversation with the same people may be enough to shift the dynamic and elicit more positive energy.

Just be aware that you may meet with resistance from family and friends—stay connected to your intention and remain as unattached to the outcome as possible. You may find that your "friends" are not really interested in supporting you changing.

Unfortunately, fitting into a group is often about everyone staying the same.

Work Relationships

I realize that I have already discussed work in the previous section, but because work is such a "charged" place, I feel it is important to look at this environment a little more closely. Work relationships tend to be especially tricky as you begin to change. Many friendships or alliances at work are built on agreements that may no longer serve you.

Just be aware of how you present yourself at work. If you suddenly start advertising your growth, you may meet with negativity or even hostility. If you stop engaging in complaining or gossiping because you recognize the negative impact these behaviors have on your growth, you may find yourself the object of gossip or criticism.

In work relationships, just as in personal relationships, there is a lot of pressure to fit in; if you simply stop going to lunch with one group or another, it can be viewed as a threat. The pecking order can begin to feel very oppressive as you shift into your personal authority. Often the first couple of weeks or months of this type of program can be very challenging—plan to use the tools from the process to stay grounded and centered when you experience upheaval around you. This may not be easy, but in the long run, it is well worth it. Remember that one of the big keys to being successful is to observe your reactions in these situations with compassion.

It is important to have an understanding of other people's perspectives but not to get caught up in their drama.

Exercise: Designing a Game Plan

It helps to have a game plan—to think through some of the possible scenarios that might arise out of your commitment to doing things differently. In this exercise, I want you to identify some "hot spots"—areas or people in your life where it might be easy to "go unconscious" and slip into patterns of behavior.

I also want you to identify some "safe zones"—areas or people with whom you feel safe. Establish who might be allies and find places where you feel comfortable "being yourself."

Lastly, I want you to write a successful strategy. This can be a general overview of your basic plan to consciously manipulate circumstances to meet your needs.

Note: Later in the book, we will be working with a specific tool aimed at addressing particularly challenging people, events, and/or environments that tend to be "charged." (The example used in the book relates to Christmas.)

25.
Detaching from Other People's Emotions and Managing Your Energy

Getting Personal: That Nun Is Crazy

Sister Mary Jean was the meanest woman I had ever met. I was in the fifth grade and new to Saint Monica's Grammar School. As the new kid, I was an easy target. It seems ludicrous to speak about a teacher, let alone a nun, looking for targets, but "Sister Mary Mean," as we called her, was a bully.

I can't remember exactly what I had said. Ultimately it was a stretch for her to take offense, but she gave herself 100 percent to her interpretation that I was being impertinent. I remember being shocked as she came after me.

She liked to get physical—she was a "hitter." She grabbed me by the arm and tried to pull me up out of my desk—they were single-unit desks with a metal bar that connected the seat to a storage compartment with a writing surface on top. My knees got caught in the crook of the bar where it bent and attached to the desktop, and I unintentionally dragged the desk with me a few feet as she tugged on me. Sister Mary Jean interpreted this as resistance and proceeded to slam me down into my seat then jerk me back up several times till I pulled free of the desk. I don't remember her hitting me, just grabbing at me frantically in various places—she got hold of my ear, my hair, the collar of my shirt. I was totally passive, but Sister Mary Jean would have made an excellent professional wrestler, as she manipulated the action to make it seem as if I was fighting back.

In the hallway, she verbally accosted me, letting me know that she would not tolerate any "clowning around" in her music appreciation class. I was totally overwhelmed and burst into tears. Her interpretation of what I had said was so preposterous, it was hard to try to defend myself. But I was (and still am) a talker. Little did I know that responding to any of her accusations tended to just make matters worse. Sister Mary Jean was only just getting going (I later learned just how long she could rant) when the principle appeared.

Sister Bernadette was a kind little old nun. She knew Sister Mary Jean was nuts, so she interceded and brought me to the office under the auspices that pulling me out of class would serve as punishment. It took a while for me to calm down and stop crying. Sister Bernadette was kind, assuring me that everything would be okay.

After I had calmed down, Sister Bernadette proceeded to give me a wonderful lesson about how best to deal with Sister Mary Jean. It reminds me of one of my life coaching sessions. She confirmed, in discreet language, of course, that Sister Mary Jean was nuts. She gave me marvelous tips on when and how to "steer clear" of Sister

Mary Jean. She helped me develop a strategy for "getting on her good side"—she mentioned that I might want to ask Sister Mary Jean about joining the choir. "You don't have to join it; just inquire about it," she suggested. In the end, we both laughed, she game me a piece of candy, and when the bell rang, she sent me out to recess.

Don't Take it Personally

You might understand intellectually that just because someone is angry, it doesn't necessarily mean that *you have done something wrong*. However, emotionally, you may still find yourself reacting to other people's anger.

You may try to make things right, even though it's not really your problem. Or you may react with anger yourself. If nothing else, you may simply let it bother you, taking you out of your present-moment experience and throwing your conscious mind into worry.

Your reactions are relatively normal, but tracking your reactions and making choices are signs of emotional maturity. Instead of unconsciously reacting as if the other person's emotions are related to you personally, your observer allows you to view the situation from a higher perspective, recognizing the situation more clearly, and consciously "unplugging" from the dynamic.

If you can track your experience, observe your reaction, apply compassion, and unplug from the other person or people energetically, you will begin to create your own reality. In simplest terms, you will have fewer and fewer "bad days." For those of us with weight issues, this may have a major influence on our eating patterns.

What does having a typical "bad day," mean for someone who struggles with weight? Here is an equation a client of mine came up with:

Bad day = Internalized Shame = One Pint of Ice Cream = Binge Eating = Brings About Self Loathing = Depression, Isolation, Irritability (and on and on and on)

Getting Personal: Conflict as a Lesson

The above equation came out of a specific event. My client's boss, who was a screamer, got mad at her. His outburst may or may not have been directed at her—there were several other employees present, and she wasn't really sure who he was mad at. But his anger most certainly made her uncomfortable. However, it was her assumption that he was mad at her specifically that led her to "act out" in a self-destructive way. She admitted to being filled with feelings of shame and guilt. When she got home, she immediately went to the freezer and opened a new pint of ice cream. This began a downward spiral of behavior and negative consequences.

In working with this woman, at first it seemed difficult if not impossible for her not to take her boss's behavior personally. I promised her that if she checked in and connected to her unconscious reactions, she could begin to interrupt her pattern.

Within a few days, a similar event occurred. She consciously tracked her experience and made choices. When her boss "blew up," she excused herself from the situation and took a bathroom break. In the "rest"-room, she did some clearing breaths. Later, when she got home, she wrote in her journal about the event. She realized that her boss's outburst triggered feelings of fear and inadequacy that came from her childhood. She reframed the experience as an opportunity to do some deep healing work around the interpretation of the little girl living inside of her. Memories came flushing back, and she saw how her pattern had developed. She used her tools to apply compassion to herself.

In her journal, she began a dialogue with the little girl inside of her. She brought her adult woman, with incredible wisdom, into the conversation. Later, I helped her identify this "adult wise woman" as her inner authority. This wise woman helped her "little girl" through the experience.

The next day, when she went to work, she felt a confidence she had never felt before. She began to take regular breaks to visit the "rest"-room. Over the next few weeks, she consciously called on her "adult wise woman" to stand up for the little girl inside of her. Interestingly, by managing her energy, she was able to deal far more effectively with her boss—some part of her knew what types of things "triggered" him, and she admitted to "getting something out of her position as a victim." Meanwhile, she put in a transfer request, and by the month's end, she was moved to a different department.

Prior to leaving, she reported having a very interesting conversation with her boss. She acknowledged her part in the dynamic they had both created and took responsibility for her reactions. She discovered that her boss could be a lot more reasonable than she had previously believed him capable of being. On some level, he understood that the two of them had created the dynamic (those weren't necessarily his words), and at some point he actually apologized for having yelled at her in the past. She honestly thanked him for everything he had taught her. They parted on amicable terms.

Becoming More Real

For my client, connecting with her emotional history allowed her to uncover a lifelong pattern. She began to have compassion for the part of her that felt inadequate, scared, overwhelmed, etc. By applying forgiveness to the part of her that judges herself, she began to change. I like to say "she became more real." This is not a quick fix, but it is a way out of the "hell of our own creation." No part of our experience is bad—by having compassion and learning to nurture and take care of ourselves, we become more human. This is a big part of becoming the best you that you can possibly be.

Managing Your Energy

The next important step in the Service to Self™ process involves learning how to manage your energy.

As you become more real and learn to take care of yourself, you may find it hard to interact in the world in the same way. It will not only be important to "unplug" energetically from dynamics that no longer serve you, but it will important to manage your energy.

Reclaiming Your Life Force

With a personal process that allows you to "be real" (accept yourself deeply and care for yourself), you will likely find that you have a lot more energy. I refer to this as reclaiming your life force.

You may recognize that your old cycles of withholding and defensiveness sapped your energy. Your lack of energy may have led to lethargy and disorganization, which may have affected your performance at work and your ability to be "present" with friends or loved ones. You may also uncover a direct relationship to eating patterns. Your new vitality may shift your life experience dramatically.

If circumstances arise and you find yourself right back in old patterns, you now have the skills to interrupt the patterns and bring yourself back to a place of "wholeness" and "well-being." You can begin to make choices around managing your energy that help shift your experience so that challenging circumstances occur far less frequently.

Manage Your Stress

When it feels like there is too much demand without appropriate perspective or relief (self-acceptance or positive self-talk, reframing or taking a learning perspective), the result is stress. Stress is a major cause of anxiety and negative self-talk, and it is often a primary cause of unconscious eating. Stress is a byproduct of not taking care of yourself (managing your energy effectively).

Doing morning meditation, taking walks at lunch, posting affirmations and reading them—these are all ways to manage your energy, focusing your attention in a positive manner.

Play is also important. Be sure you have healthy outlets to let loose. Be cautious of ways you may have learned to "blow off steam" that don't rejuvenate you (such as drinking alcohol).

Choose your vacations wisely—it is very easy for vacations to become stressful instead of being relaxing or rejuvenating. Trying to plan or cram too much into a vacation can make you more "stressed out" than being home or at work.

Ultimately, we are talking about choice. You now have a process for examining your choices to determine if the results are beneficial or if a different choice might actually serve you better. By making conscious choices and changing habits that no longer work for your life, you will find yourself a lot happier and more fulfilled. And you will invariably make different choices around food.

If you have trouble making self-honoring choices, it is a good indication to look deeper, as we have done throughout the book, at the underlying emotions and conditioned beliefs that make such changes so difficult. You may want to check out the agreements and beliefs that are making it so hard to manage your energy.

Exercise: Tracking Choices and Managing Energy
In this chapter, we have discussed energy and vitality. There are three things I want you to explore over the next week.

The first is to consciously unplug from some energy that you recognize is no longer working for you. Perhaps it is an activity, perhaps it is a relationship—just try limiting the time you spend doing the activity or interacting with the particular person. Write in you journal about the effect this choice has on your vitality.

For the second component, I want you to examine what effect self-honoring choices have on your energy level. Each day, focus on one minor adjustment and see what the effect is on your sense of well-being. For example: Monday I posted three affirmations (one on my computer at work, one on my mirror in the bathroom, and one on the dashboard of my car). Tuesday I added a twenty-minute walk during my lunch break. Wednesday I …

The third step is to use an exercise called "Clearing Breaths" to focus your energy and literally bring vitality into your body through your breath. This can be done several times a day. (I once had a client who set the timer on his watch to beep once every hour during his day to remind him to "breathe.") If you can, find a quiet place to close your eyes (this may mean simply closing your office door, or it may involve getting up and going somewhere—I find "rest"-room stalls work wonderfully).

You are going to be taking three to five clearing breaths—this should only take a few minutes. Close your eyes and take some long, deep, clearing breaths. Slowly breathe in through the nose, hold for a few seconds, then slowly release the breath out through the mouth. Hold for a few seconds, then repeat. Let the thoughts drift away; give yourself permission to let go. If it helps, gently remind yourself that it is only a few minutes. Let the breath coming in give you energy and restore you. Allow the release of your breath to clear your mind, releasing any demand, any negativity, or any chatter.

I realize that this is the last thing you feel like doing when you are experiencing stress, but I assure you it is the best way to interrupt the stress and help you deal with whatever challenging circumstances are present.

Note: Because this exercise is especially useful in stressful environments, I do it in the car on my way to and from meetings, appointments, dropping the kids off, etc. I find that red lights are usually the perfect amount of time to take three clearing breaths. (Close your eyes and don't worry about the light turning green; the driver behind you will usually let you know when the light changes.)

I also find that just doing one or two clearing breath whenever I am about to eat changes the pace at which I consume my food. I tend to not only eat slower, but I often eat less – simply because I am calmer, I am paying attention to my body and I have activated my ability to make choices.

> If you don't go within, you go without. —Proverb

In your journal, report what you discover Unplugging from Negativity and Managing Your Energy.

26.
Practice Becomes Habit—
Healing the Split

Getting Personal: Date Night

I say that my relationship with myself, my relationship with my wife, and my relationship with my children are my priorities. However, jobs, bills, chores, errands, and obligations seem to dominate my life to the point where it is easy to forget to honor my relationship with myself, let alone find time to connect with my loved ones. I find the relationship with my wife to be especially important, but also especially challenging. It feels as if each of us is split into little pieces and our lives are compartmentalized into roles we play in order to just get through each day.

At this point in our lives, both my wife and I recognize that we must consciously implement strategic choices on a regular basis, to stay connected—both individually and as a couple.

I recognize how easy the above statement is to make, but how hard it can actually be to arrive at self-honoring choices. It is very easy to fall into a "rut" and develop habits that don't serve us. My wife and I recently found ourselves "hooked" on some silly reality show that comes on too late in the evening and doesn't provide much "upliftment." We justified it by saying that we just wanted to "check out" and be entertained.

Ultimately, checking out is fine, but my wife and I also need time to check in, so that we maintain a quality relationship. We need to examine our choices, individually and collectively, to determine if we are really getting enough fulfillment out of the activities we are engaged in. Often, this is a process where it takes a series of choices to develop a truly honoring routine.

The following story illustrates one such example:

Once a week, my wife and I have "date night," where we get a babysitter and do something as a couple. Initially, we used this time to go to a movie. But we discovered that going to the movies didn't help us connect with one another, so we shifted to going to a nice dinner. But after a short time, we recognized that having a bottle of wine and overeating were not serving our relationship or our individual well-being. So, we decided to skip the alcohol, eat at healthier restaurants, and consciously under-order, so that we didn't overeat. Without the booze and with less food, we found dinner ended much quicker and we had an hour or two to spend after we finished eating. Initially, we began using this time to shop or run errands, until we recognized that this was not a truly beneficial use of the valuable time.

One day at dinner, my wife suggested we check out a local yoga studio. We had both attempted yoga in the past, but neither of us stuck with it. The yoga was very hard at first, and some part of me didn't want to do it. But both Jasmine and I committed to this positive choice, and we have been doing it ever since. Over time, we have come to love it. We now also go to yoga on Sunday mornings. In addition, each of us tries to attend at least one additional class during the week. Our yoga practice is now fully integrated into our lives.

"Date night" now involves a light, healthy dinner, a walk in the neighborhood around the yoga studio, some wonderful conversation, followed by an uplifting yoga class.

You will need to practice
Making self-honoring choices is primarily an inside job. It doesn't happen all at once—it is a process that takes practice.

When we practice something over and over again, it becomes habit. This is true of positive traits and negative beliefs. If we consistently respond to the world in a particular way, we create a habit, not just of behavior but of thinking. As you show compassion for yourself and begin to address your needs directly, your habits begin to change. You will find yourself making adjustments that honor your intention and add fulfillment to your life.

As you begin to trust what you know about yourself, you gain confidence from identifying and observing the patterns that are limiting you. You begin to consciously act on your newfound discoveries to accentuate your strengths and *reframe* your perceived deficiencies.

In your self-observation, you may have begun to recognize that your perceived weaknesses (for which you shame and blame yourself) are based on misinterpretations. You may discover that what you've assumed are personal flaws were actually programmed, usually early in childhood, by other people. As you move out of a defensive persona into authenticity, you will come to discover that your vulnerability provides a wisdom and sensitivity that can truly serve you.

A growing inner sense of self-worth, an inner authority, will begin to direct your life, and it will become easier and easier to make self-honoring choices.

The Split

Being authentic is not a switch we simply flip on and it stays on—you may find yourself falling back into a persona, especially under certain circumstances.

Persona is a constructed sense of self (I referred to it earlier in this book as the "false self"), which we began to develop in early childhood. All of us found people we wanted to emulate. Our personality formed in order to protect ourselves or make ourselves feel better. We developed a false self. The authentic self, which lies underneath the persona, has been judged and relegated to a secondary position. Often when people begin to heal, they experience what I call "the split." It is as if there are two different people within them.

Like putting on a mask, a person may act in a certain way in public or at work (the persona or false self), then drop the mask and act in a totally different way (authentic self) when they feel as if they are in a safe environment. This split between the authentic self and the false self can exist for a very long time. Healing the split requires developing your inner authority and accessing it regularly. You are simply learning how to be more and more authentic in a variety of different environments.

I see this as a process of integration. It does not happen overnight; in fact, it often takes years, if not a lifetime. Finding authentic ways to "show up" in environments that seem hostile or difficult is a great challenge. It takes courage and a commitment to working one's process. However, the benefits are immeasurable. This is the basis for fulfillment. It is at this integrated level that a sense of purpose and oneness can occur.

Exercise: Practice Honoring Yourself

By accessing your inner authority and utilizing all of the Service to Self™ tools you have learned so far, you are going to develop a "practice" to honor yourself. Small, incremental shifts in behavior will lay the groundwork for creating habits that change the quality of your life and lead to becoming the "you" that you were born to be. This process is especially effective when working with a partner, because another level of accountability is introduced.

The goal of this exercise is to stretch out of one's comfort zone little by little. Many bad habits are simply born out of unconscious behaviors repeated over time. The idea is to meet personal needs by making self-honoring choices in a manner that becomes a practice. The positive behaviors in the practice, when repeated over a long enough period of time, become positive habits. These positive behaviors should be small action steps that you commit to. It is important that the action steps are simply minor adjustments in your life. If the practice is too ambitious, you may get overwhelmed and it will be hard to stick with it.

Here is an example for each of the three levels (mind, spirit, body) we will be working on.

For the "mind" stretch, I might start or join a book club.

For spirit, I might commit to listening to spiritual CDs (minimum of ten minutes, three days a week).

For body, I might go for a hike (at least once a week, for at least forty minutes).

A great way to begin is by committing to "the practice" for two weeks. Again, this process is most effective when working with a partner.

The following table is downloadable at www.servicetoself.com

My Practice to Honor Myself	Mon.	Tue.	Wed.	Thu.	Fri.	Sat.	Sun.
Mind							
Body							
Spirit							

27.
Correcting Your Course

Getting Personal: You Can Change Your Mind

"You can change your mind, you know." Walter and I were near the top of the mountain when he said this to me. It was as if a light suddenly went off in my brain. Hiking along that afternoon, I began to realize that I had bought into some warped sense of commitment. Somewhere in my psyche, it was as if there was a voice saying, "You made your bed, kid, and now you have to lie in it." I'm not sure whose voice it was, telling me that, but I had received the message that once you make a commitment, you cannot go back on your word.

On that crisp spring day eleven years ago, near the top of the mountain, I changed my mind. The course my life was taking was not working for me. I wanted to take a different path—I was going to ask for a divorce.

By the time I reached the top of the summit, my world had opened up—and as I gazed over the breathtaking landscape, I knew what I had to do—I was clear for the first time in years.

Correcting the Course

Creating a practice to honor yourself may not seem so challenging. Just reading it, it may appear easy, but everyone I know who has tried to do it has met with resistance. Remember, there is no such thing as failure—when you meet with resistance, it simply means that there is an opportunity to learn. From a learning perspective, utilize your resistance as an opportunity to grow.

There is tremendous growth involved in noting your inner conflict and working with it to get back on course. Give the resistance a voice and let it teach you. Then recommit to the action step.

Remember that you are still developing a conscious compassionate observer. It is critical to use this tool to work through the issues that arise. Observe how your reactive mind responds to resistance. Catch self-judgment and use checking-in techniques to keep yourself on course.

Judging the Judge

A common pitfall that many people fall into when they begin tracking their judgments involves reacting to the judgments they discover. It is important to understand the purpose of judgment in your life, so that you can move into acceptance. Acceptance is the first step in releasing judgment.

The challenge is to work *with* the inner critic. Most people judge the critic, not recognizing that its purpose was to protect them from getting hurt. This can be especially difficult when you identify a source for the negative beliefs—say, a parent.

When cautionary or critical words get internalized as limitations, it is hard not to blame the source of the misinformation. Judgment blocks healing, so compassion must be applied to all parties in the misunderstanding that have led to the negative beliefs. You must face your inner critic with compassion and release any blame associated with its source.

Any part of yourself that you deny becomes a hindrance to your growth and healing. Every part of your experience is lovable. Love and compassion help you acknowledge your humanity in all of your life experiences. You can turn perceived weaknesses into sources of power and strength as you gain the wisdom that comes from embracing your experience.

This is especially important when you catch yourself in a negative pattern around food. It is imperative that you don't slip into self-criticism on any level. The negative eating pattern simply occurred in order to alert you to something that is going on for you that needs to be recognized and addressed. If judgment comes up, thank your inner-critic for trying to protect and help you, then gently release your judgment using self-forgiveness. Remember to get to "and the truth is", because this is where the deeper issue gets recognized.

Exercise: Make One Change

Over the next week, I want you to consider a change that you want to make. This could be as simple as moving some furniture around. Try to pick something that you have some resistance to changing—but don't make it a huge step. For this exercise I don't want you to pick anything that is directly related to food, diet or exercise. I want you to write in you journal about the process.

28.
Choosing Our Reality

What You Can Learn from the Moken Tribe

In December of 2004, a tsunami hit the coast of Thailand, killing an estimated 300,000 people. The Moken tribe lived on islands off the coast, which were supposedly hit the hardest. Their villages were destroyed, but no one died. This astounding outcome got the attention of the TV program *60 Minutes,* which sent a correspondent out to investigate. What the news crew discovered was a group of people who experience reality profoundly differently than those of us living in the Western world.

Moken don't know how old they are, because they don't measure time; in fact, they have no word for "when." *When* is not the only word missing from the Moken language. *Want* is another. They believe material things tie you down. They have no notion or desire for wealth. It just so happens that this tribe is under constant threat from the Burmese government, which has taken over several of their islands and turned them into military bases. But the Moken don't seem terribly worried by this. Perhaps that's because *worry* is just one more of those words that don't exist in their language. They also don't have words for "hello" and "goodbye."

The reason no one died in the Tsunami is because the Moken moved to higher ground just prior to the Tsunami hitting the islands. Similar to Native Americans, the Moken live in harmony with the natural world. They honor it and cherish it, and they have learned to pay attention to it. When the weather changed and the sea went completely calm, they knew it was an indication that something was wrong. The animals on the island began to move to higher ground, and the Moken, trusting their instinct, did the same.

The truth is that the Moken literally live in a different mental and spiritual reality.

In the case of the Moken, their unique world view prevents many problems and neuroses. Clearly they don't spend time worrying about their age, their possessions, or many of the other "problems" that we obsess about in our "advanced" Western civilization.

> We don't see things as they are, we see things as we are. —Anais Nin

The story of the Moken illustrates the concept that reality is interpretive. What is real or important to you may not be conceivable to a Moken, because the Moken are programmed differently. Your culture or tribal history constitutes your "programming." You have been conditioned to view the world in a particular way, but your perceptions are subjective.

Understanding that our programming greatly influences our perception, we can begin to observe "our reality." The question is: Can we reprogram? Do we need to go back in time or can we make adjustments right now that begin to shift our beliefs? Can we re-design our reality?

The way you perceive the world is "reality" as you know it. The problem with most processes is that they tend to focus too heavily on negative perceptions, without a mechanism for changing or shifting beliefs. Put simply, people focus too much energy on their "problems" rather than channeling their energy into *reframing* the situation and thereby moving naturally into a solution. This process is about replacing beliefs that are not working in your life with positive beliefs that lead to fulfillment. You are ultimately choosing your reality.

Remember the Observer

You are developing a new muscle utilizing the conscious compassionate observer to nurture an inner authority. This can take you out of the world of problems and into a new reality.

The conscious compassionate observer allows you to consider other points of view. Understanding that shame, blame, and guilt are misinterpretations helps to reshape your perception of reality. By living in the mode of conscious observation and practicing *acceptance* (not resisting or judging your perceptions or actions), you will find that your day-to-day experience becomes much more fulfilling.

Positive input is going to replace negative input—and you will begin to reprogram your reality.

Unplug from Negative Sources

Remember that there is a lot of support in this culture for your negative perceptions. Choose where you get your information—again, you may want to be careful reading the paper and watching TV—they tend to promote fear and negativity. The Service to Self™ process involves tracking your experience in every area of your life to see what is truly bringing you fulfillment and what no longer supports you.

Exercise:
Using Your Journal to Explore a New Quality of Life

Choose one of the following minor adjustments to your present routine and write in your journal about the effect it has on the quality of your life. Or make up your own minor adjustment based on shifting from a pattern that supports programmed messages to a behavior that promotes positive messages in your consciousness.

1) If you presently watch the news prior to going to bed, try turning off the TV at least one hour before sleep and reading an uplifting book, taking a bath, or listening to soothing music. Track how you feel in the morning by writing in your journal notebook for five minutes.

2) If you read magazines during your breaks at work or while on the train going to the office, try replacing this material with something positive. (Note: even if you are careful to only read the positive articles, the advertising and layout can promote or reinforce a negative self-image.)

3) If you read the newspaper every day, replace it with an uplifting book.

Uplifting books I recommend for this process:

- *Tuesdays with Morrie* by Mitch Albom
- *The Bridge Across Forever* by Richard Bach
- *The Alchemist* by Paulo Coelho
- *View more suggestions at www.servicetoself.com*

4) If you rent movies, choose movies with positive messages such as:

- *The Kid*
- *Pay it Forward*
- *Life Is Beautiful*
- *Benny and Joon*
- *Billy Elliot*
- *View more suggestions at www.servicetoself.com*

I will bet that doing the above exercise for a week has a profound effect on your experience. Beyond this exercise, pay particular attention to direct messages that you have integrated into your daily routine that promote the critical voice within you. This may include jokes you send and receive over e-mail. (Just delete them—don't participate in the negativity.)

The world around you isn't going to suddenly stop sending out negative messages, but you can begin to track your experience and make positive choices.

When things get overwhelming, go for self-*support;* take a walk, listen to uplifting music, meditate. Try to cultivate a more objective view of the world and of yourself. This is sometimes referred to as "equanimity," or taking an impersonal perspective on life and *accepting* things as they are.

(Note: Equanimity is a central concept of Buddhist meditation practice. It is a major theme, for example, in *The Art of Happiness: A Handbook for Living* by the Dalai Lama and Howard C. Cutler. See appendix.)

From a place of equanimity, visualization and affirmations are tools to keep your thoughts focused on the positive, and "tuned in" to a higher frequency where understanding, compassion, and tolerance come naturally.

As you nurture a positive view of yourself and the world around you, your relationship with food and with your body will change.

Remember, reactions and emotions are not good or bad—they are simply information. Think of them as opportunities to check in, learn, and grow—to become a more compassionate human being, and ultimately to find peace and fulfillment by getting your needs met, giving your gifts, and being of service.

29.
The Power of Perception

Getting Personal: Value Doesn't Depend on Currency

When I was in Czechoslovakia in 1985, the country was under Communist rule. The Czechoslovakian currency was virtually worthless—all the Czech people wanted were deutschmarks or dollars. What was remarkable was that people with skills, talents, and abilities that were valuable still got paid—they simply used other currencies or traded goods and services using a barter system.

Perceived Value

Take out a dollar and look at it; it is a piece of paper with ink. The value is perceived. The anxiety that people are feeling as a result of the financial crisis of 2008–2009 (during which time this book is being written) comes from the general perception that the value of their life savings and hard work is being diminished and may disappear altogether. This can easily lead to a nightmarish negative future fantasy.

At this point we still agree, along with the rest of the world, that the dollar has value, so it does. The fact is that the dollar is a Federal Reserve note—a loan—not tied to anything. In the past, there was the gold standard and the silver certificate, but today there is nothing backing it except a general perception of value. It is an illusion to which we have collectively agreed.

I have mentioned several times that losing all of the wealth I accumulated as a real estate developer became a tremendous gift to me. I realize that my skills, talents, and abilities are real— my monetized net worth was an illusion. Many of my friends and colleges in the development world have been very slow to recover from the economic crisis. It is my opinion that many of them are still caught up in the illusion, and moving on in their lives has been especially difficult based on their emotional and psychological investment in the belief that they have somehow lost something or something has been taken away.

Exercise: My New Net Worth

The financial documents that companies use to track the value of their institution have a line item called "goodwill." A dollar figure is assigned to this item. The value of the goodwill is a measurement of the positive relationships that company has in the marketplace, as well as the positive image the brand represents to the consumer.

In your journal, I want you to create a Personal Value Statement—a balance sheet, if you will. You may want to do this as an Excel file, but you can just as easily draw some lines in your journal to fill out the categories. Anyone experiencing uncertainty or fear around their personal economic situation may find this exercise especially important.

Create a category called "assets." I want you to "line item" each of your assets—by assets, I don't mean stocks, bonds, or real estate—I mean personal qualities that bring value to whatever you invest your energy in. For example: "I am friendly and outgoing"—would be a line item, and I would place a dollar figure on what that quality should be worth in the marketplace.

Create a category called "liabilities." Here I want you to list the limiting beliefs and unhealthy patterns that devalued you.

Once you are finished, calculate your true net worth—realize we are using dollars as a metaphor.

Now, if you really want security in your life, work on yourself. Doing the Service to Self™ process may be the greatest financial investment you have ever made. I can virtually assure you that whatever happens to the economy, your chance of surviving the downturn and finding success and fulfillment will go up greatly if you go about investing in your assets and curing your liabilities.

30.
Creating More Practices to Care for Yourself and Heal

Getting Personal: It Feels Good

In my high school, all the students were required to do 100 hours of community service over four years. Initially, this seemed like a huge drag, and I didn't want to do it. I couldn't see how community service had anything to do with learning. I interpreted the requirement as a way of manipulating Catholic high school kids to do a bunch of free work for Catholic charities.

Little did I know what a profound impact and a tremendous gift this requirement would end up being for me in my life. All of my community service activities gave me opportunities to bring my valuable skills to worthy causes. I got to practice kindness as I mentored young kids—I felt great about myself by giving encouragement and support to others. Ultimately, my service work allowed me to network my way into a long-term summer job whenever I was out of school, ultimately leading to a flexible part-time job when I graduated from college.

Expanding Your Practices

You have made a series of adjustments to your behavior patterns and begun to reframe problems and setbacks as opportunities for growth. Now you will want to develop practices that incorporate your new consciousness, along with your talents, skills, and abilities in ways that serve the "you" you were born to be.

The following practices are designed to help accentuate the compassion and acceptance you have found for yourself, by bringing your gifts into relationship with others as you become aligned with your authentic self.

Practicing Kindness

By now, you may have noticed yourself being nicer to others. This is an inevitable result of practicing self-acceptance and compassion for yourself—it naturally makes you kinder and more compassionate in the world.

This is more than just fulfilling, it is smart. Research actually demonstrates that kindness has a positive physiological effect on your body. Scientist have been able to measure Serotonin levels in peoples brains (Serotonin is a chemical in the brain that is related to feeling good) around acts of kindness. Not only does being kind increase production of Serotonin, but also witnessing kindness increases Serotonin levels. Even hearing about an act of kindness elevates the levels of Serotonin in test patients.

Getting Personal: The world opens up with possibilities

One client told me that by doing the Service to Self Program™, he opened up and began to change how he treated others, in surprising ways. He provided an incredibly simple example of the shift he was experiencing.

At a coffee shop near his home, there was a waitress to whom he had never spoken other than to order his food. He noticed that she had a different hairstyle, one that was especially flattering. In the past, he confessed, "I was so self-absorbed, I never would have noticed that." He mentioned his observation to her and gave her a sincere compliment. He saw how it brightened her day, but he also noticed, and said to himself, *What the heck is going on? I never do stuff like this.* He realized that he was changing. He left the restaurant that morning feeling great, and he proceeded to have a terrific day.

As we have mentioned before, internally each of us has two sides—we have an inner critic and we have an inner supporter. This person was managing to develop his inner supporter to view the world from a positive perspective, resulting in significant personal transformation.

Remember, our practice is about quieting the inner critic and nurturing the inner supporter. Here is how it works: What you believe is what you perceive. The way you perceive the world is "reality" as you know it. But as you change your perception, the world around you shifts—the sky gets a little brighter, the trees a little greener, the flowers more vibrant—a "life force" begins to move in and around you based on your outlook. The world changes in front of your eyes.

Exercise: Find an Opportunity to Be Kind to Someone
I want you to go out in the world looking for an opportunity to be kind to someone. Don't force it; just hold the intention in your consciousness to be kind—an opportunity will surely arise.

After you have completed your act of kindness, I want you to write in your journal about your experience.

Practice Creating Value

A big part of our self-worth tends to come from work. Our society (what I refer to as our tribe) promotes the Protestant work ethic—hard work equals a life well-lived. But in our society, we often measure our work by monetary results; remember how I measured my success only by my bank account. Note: you may also have been measuring your worth with your bathroom scale.

But when we orient ourselves to creating value in the world, we set ourselves up for a different kind of success.

You should never think about being paid for time, but rather look to spend your time creating value. Instead of thinking, *How much will I make in an hour?* instead think, *How much value can I create in one hour?*

People who create value tend to be compensated accordingly. When it is time for a company to lay people off, those who have become especially valuable are often spared the pink slip. When it is time to promote someone, those who create the most value are often given the higher position because they are an asset to the company (based on the assets they bring to the table—look at your balance sheet and consider what assets you bring to your job and which assets you might be withholding).

But a practice of creating value reflects inside as well. If you know you have not done your best and have essentially cheated or short-changed your employer, partner, or customer, it takes its toll on your self-image, and it will weaken your inner authority. You will feel like a fraud.

Only you know, inside yourself, if you've done your best and created value. Sometimes our inability to do our best is the result of limiting beliefs ("I'm not good enough"). Or it may be the result of a victim consciousness, within a cycle of blaming others or looking for external causes or obstacles that we use as an excuse—we have become complainers rather than achievers.

By keeping the focus inside and doing your best, you will certainly create value, both externally and internally—you will strengthen your inner authority, promoting an internal sense of competence.

Exercise: Value Added

In the next week, I want you to focus on adding value. Set a strong intention. Look at your assets and find ways to bring those assets into relationship with others.

Then I want you to write in your journal about the experience.

Practice Praising

Noticing people's strengths is far better than focusing on their weaknesses. As you move into leading with your own strengths, it is very important to begin to notice other people's strengths as well. Look for opportunities to state your appreciation for the strengths and contributions of others.

Praising people is a wonderful way of celebrating success. When you see people as assets and you *acknowledge* their talents, gifts, and abilities, you move into alignment with your own higher self.

Recognizing the excellence of others creates an atmosphere of abundance and ease. It helps to overcome any tendency toward scarcity in your interpersonal dealings. The feelings that unfold are genuine.

Exercise: Tell People How Great They Are

In the next week or so, I want you to find opportunities to tell people how great they are. The most important part of this exercise may be your resistance. When you resist being complimentary of others, it is a strong indication that the negative voices are still "running the show" in your unconscious mind. "Feeling phony" when complimenting someone is another indication that negative self-perception is still operating within you. Work with this skill and use your journal to process any resistance that comes up.

Practice Being of Service

Being of service to others can be as rewarding as it is valuable. I have always tried to consciously be of service in different ways throughout my life. One of the ways I've done this has been through teaching. I began teaching long before I ever considered my current career. I believe that because I was in "right alignment" with my natural skills, talents, and abilities, the universe (or God) provided me with the perfect training opportunities. Besides the collateral benefits from my years of volunteering, the joy I received from my students was compensation beyond what money could have provided.

Even work that I am paid for, I view as being of service, because I am adding value to the lives of the clients I work with.

Exercise: Be of Service

Find ways—even if it is at your present job—to consciously be of service to others. I want you to write in your journal about the experience.

Practice Networking

Networking is all about building *sincere* relationships. Bonding with people from a place of sincerity is much better than trying to establish a relationship based on self-interest. And networking is not just about business. If you approach business and personal relationships from the standpoint of providing value and being of service, they will naturally become mutually beneficial.

A good way to form sincere relationships is by engaging in activities that you enjoy. If you love art, join a museum and attend openings. If you love music, find some local artists to follow. Interact with others over your sincere love for life—share your joy.

Perhaps there is something you haven't tried but feel like you might enjoy, such as yoga or swing dancing—try taking a class. Find positive environments and constructive outlets to fill your free time. Work to develop deeper connections and bonds with people over shared interests.

Exercise: Practice Networking

Take the risk to put your authentic self "out there" and meet people. Look for connections and deepen your bonds by being loving and supportive toward others. Notice their gifts, talents, and abilities, and praise them from a sincere and genuine place within yourself.

I want you to write in your journal about the experience.

Practice Mentoring or Being Mentored

I think it's great when young people find a mentor. There's an old saying that says, "When the student is ready, the teacher appears; when the teacher is ready, the student appears." I think that there is not enough respect given in the culture for teaching and learning. There is an assumption that you are supposed to do and learn everything by yourself.

This eliminates one of life's most special relationships, that of student and teacher. Having an older friend who is willing to bless us with his or her experience and knowledge is a tremendous gift. Giving of our own expertise in a positive and caring way can greatly enhance our own self-image.

I would like to encourage you to hold in your consciousness that there might be a person with a particular experience or understanding that might be willing to be of service to you, or there may be a person who could benefit from what you understand or have learned in your life.

Exercise: The Mentor

In the coming weeks, I want you to be willing to be a student of life and go out and find the master teachers to help guide you on your way. Also, as you come to a place of self-acceptance and wisdom, consider sharing what you have learned and experienced with others.

Practice Care-fronting

Part of the Service to Self™ process involves being responsible for your behavior—but it also involves holding others accountable for their behavior. If you are going to get your needs met, you must begin to ask for what you want. Clients have often misunderstood this to mean that they must begin confronting people in order to express their "truth." They often feel a sense of entitlement, stemming from the needs they are uncovering. I don't recommend confronting—but I do recommend "care-fronting."

The primary distinction between confronting and care-fronting is intention. The objective in confronting is to convince the other person that they are wrong, while the primary objective in care-fronting is to heal and grow. An example of the care-fronting dialogue may begin with something such as this: "I care about you, and I want to improve the quality of our relationship, so I would like to talk to you about what happened the other day."

The next piece is to report your experience in a non-accusatory fashion, taking responsibility for your reaction and/or behavior. This is based on the premise that the event is not the cause of the feelings, but rather the feelings existed within you, and the event simply triggered them.

For example, you might say, "I reacted the other day to something you said (or did), and I want to talk to you about it, because I don't want there to be a misunderstanding between us." You may want the other person to know that you don't intend on blaming or accusing them of anything; you just want to report your experience in an effort to have open and honest communication with them.

The next step is to report your experience without blame or accusation. You may want to include any interpretations that you are aware of, which came up during the triggering event, always letting the person know that your interpretation may or may not have been accurate.

Remember: you must understand that interpretations are always skewed based on our emotional history, core beliefs (which may or may not be accurate), and unconscious agreements (these are the dynamics we unconsciously engage in—the roles we play in a relationship). Note: It probably isn't appropriate to try to offer someone all of this information (pertaining to your interpretation). It is simply important to hold in your consciousness that your interpretation is relative. (It may or may not be accurate and it may differ greatly from the other person's interpretation.)

Try to report what it feels like to be you. Be open to the other person's experience and take in *what it feels like to be them.* "Other" can be a bit of a difficult concept to embrace, but it is critical to conflict resolution and healing to understand that *the other person is not you.* (They have their own history, beliefs and agreements.)

Do not try to "fix" anyone. Care-fronting requires that you simply hear them, empathize with them, and try to see the situation from their perspective, while being open and honest about your experience.

When you have listened carefully and absorbed the other person's experience, you may want to repeat back a few key points, so that they know that you have made an effort to hear what they have to say.

If appropriate, you might ask for what you want, but not in a demanding way—offer it for their consideration. Try to recognize a want or need that you might be able to fulfill for the other person as well.

This may well reveal a further layer of feelings on the part of the other person as they respond to your request and take in your offer. You must be prepared for any possible response, because you have recognized that their point of view is not yours.

I have found that this sort of dialogue can heal long rifts between family, friends, and co-workers.

Exercise: Try Care-fronting:
Initially, I strongly recommend that you work with this skill in the safest setting and with the easiest possible person—for example, your gardener (someone with whom you have a simple straightforward relationship). Work with this for a while before you start trying to use this tool with close personal relationships. In other words, don't call your mother whom you haven't spoken with in five years and try this—not just yet. In fact, I have included an exercise specifically designed to help with charged relationships or situations by employing a special "Ideal Vision" process, later in the book.

31.
Checking In, One Step Further

Getting Personal: Solitude

I'm a people person—I like to be around people, and I get a lot of my needs met in relationship with others. Creating a meditation practice was a hard adjustment to make in my life. Initially, I learned to meditate in a group—by joining a meditation class that met once a week. I felt like I needed to share my solitary experience with others. It was almost as if I wanted to make sure I wasn't crazy or that I wasn't alone in my experience.

Today, my mediation practice is a gift I give to myself. Solitude is not isolation—even though I sometimes feel isolated when I am alone for long periods of time. Being consistent with my mediation practice is still a tremendous challenge for me, but I recognize the value it adds to my life. When I fall off my schedule, I gently bring myself back to silence and self-forgiveness, as I venture back into wholeness through my breath.

Practice Meditation: Checking in on a Schedule

Modern quantum physics and neuroscience, as well as ancient mysticism, tell us that our reality is literally based on where we place our attention. The "new science" is proving what the mystical traditions have told us for thousands of years—that the observer (or consciousness) greatly influences what occurs in the physical world.

Meditation is one of the ancient practices that has demonstrated its effectiveness over many centuries, to connect a person to higher energy and being.

Remember that we have discussed the fact that the power of intention and affirmation has a scientific basis. Bringing these elements into your meditation practice can produce powerful results. But the essence of most meditation is observation rather than control, so introduce your intentions and affirmations gently, allowing the unfolding of events and circumstances their natural course.

While meditation may seem mysterious, if you've followed the process in this book, you've already done it. Many of the exercises have involved "checking in." You've been prompted to pay attention to your breath.

Some meditative practices involve using a "mantra," or specific sound, and keeping one's attention focused.

The how or even the why of meditation doesn't matter at all. In fact, the how and the why are part of what is being observed during meditation: your conscious thoughts.

The key to the process is being "mindful"—which essentially means not getting lost in thoughts about the past or future, but keeping one's attention in the present and thereby connecting (checking in) to one's body.

When you are mindful, aware of your thoughts but not caught in them, as well as connected to your body, you will make different choices around food.

There are many books and resources that teach meditation, but again the *how* is not important. The two most important aspects of meditation are not to look for results or judge how you're doing, and then to simply meditate on a regular and committed basis.

Let me stress that you do not need to "study" meditation or really even learn it. Use the process of checking in to connect deeply with the sensations that seem to hold tension, and be present. Sit with the sensations and even negativity, if necessary, for brief periods of time (five to ten minutes when you first begin, and fifteen to twenty minutes after you have been mediating for a period of time). Let yourself release the negative energy with your exhaling breath and bring in new energy and vitality on every inhale.

If thoughts intrude, gently let them flow on through. I often like to imagine a stream; the thoughts are like tiny bubbles appearing in the stream. I watch them for a moment, then they pop or drift gently downstream and out of view.

If you follow this practice regularly, as part of preparing for and completing each day, you will find that your ability to step back and observe your conditioned mind improves, along with many of your external circumstances.

Exercise: Your Meditation Practice

Releasing weight, in my opinion, is almost dependent on quieting the mind. Start with just five minutes in the morning and five minutes at night. Also know that many activities can take on a meditative quality just by working to quiet the mind. (I find doing the dishes especially meditative.) Walking meditation, especially in nature, can be incredibly soothing and centering—just practice breathing and being in the present moment, allowing the thoughts to just drift through your consciousness as you focus on being one with the natural environment.

Whatever you choose to do, write down your commitment in your journal and track your progress and resistance. Think of meditation as a gift you give yourself.

32.
A Tool for Shifting Difficult Dynamics and Challenging Circumstances

Getting Personal: Christmas Dinner

The example used in this chapter comes directly from my life—it is the ideal vision I did before going to Christmas dinner with my family in 2008.

Christmas has always been a "charged" holiday for me. Through my personal process, I have come to recognize how needy I feel around the holiday. I am also particularly sensitive—often finding myself offended by the littlest comment or circumstance. In the past I tended to eat and drink way too much.

On this particular Christmas, I did an ideal vision. The results were tremendous. Every "action item" I listed to focus my energy worked out beautifully. On the few occasions where I felt myself slipping into unconscious behavior, I removed myself from the situation, went to a quiet place (the "rest"-room) and re-read my vision. I had an amazing, loving, and fulfilling experience.

Exercise: Visualizing Intentions for a "Charged" Event

In this exercise, you will visualize various scenarios for a potentially stressful event. This exercise will allow you to transform what you have previously considered a problem into an opportunity for activating many of the positive emotions and new patterns that have emerged through your process.

Since the process is visual, use the following diagram as a basis for your own drawing, or if you have a program like Word, PowerPoint, or Visio, you could use the drawing tools to replicate the diagram below and work with those tools.

(Only use the computer if you are proficient in the appropriate program; do not let your efforts to build the diagram "correctly," on the computer hamper your heartfelt processes. If you find yourself looking up "Help" on the computer, it's probably better to work with pen and paper.)

In the example, I used my Christmas dinner with family, many of whom "push my buttons" and trigger negative reactions.

Try to find one main intention statement that you can repeat in your head over the course of the event. Use the boxes to write out how you *intend* to meet your needs and relate to others. Explore what type of experience you are intending to manifest. Be strategic in addressing the quality of experience you wish to have. Be sure to address the various "button-pushers" you will likely encounter.

Christmas dinner provides an excellent frame of reference for this exercise because of the patterns and reactions it tends to evoke.

The occasion tends to induce a lot of negative self-talk, and we tend to comfort ourselves with food—only to regret it later.

As you construct your own vision, refer to the diagram to guide you. This may take several drafts.

Okay, now here's the example of a fully filled-in diagram from my own *experience:*

Freeman's Ideal Vision of Xmas '08

Intention Statement: My Intention this Christmas is to work to stay clear, make connections, meet my needs consciously and be of loving service

Connection

I am checking in with my wife to be sure we are staying connected

I am reaching out to my brother in a loving way

I am sharing one-on-one time with Grandma - knowing that this may be her last Christmas

Needs

I am staying grounded and centered by taking short breaks throughout the evening and consciously moving by breath

I am going to my wife periodically and connecting with her physically

Service

I am spending time with the children helping them channel their excitement

I am being helpful in the kitchen - possibly carving the meat

I am making sure Grandma gets taken care of

Clarity

My wife and I are making decisions as a team

I am checking in with my intention - to be of loving service to my family

I am seeing the loving essence of all family members - even those whom I struggle with

I surrender my limited vision to a higher intelligence for the greatest good

Notice at the bottom the statement "I surrender my limited vision to a higher intelligence, for the greatest good." This statement is very important—the spiritual principle of acceptance allows for the natural unfolding of our lives. We do not want to try to "over-direct" our lives. This vision represents your best intention—but the unfolding may be different than you might expect—allow for that unfolding and trust your intention.

You can use your completed diagram in a number of ways. (The exercise is not over when you complete the diagram.)

Look at the diagram before you do your checking-in process, particularly before attending the event.

Take it with you to the event as a reminder of your intentions toward the various people or circumstances you referred to in the scenarios. You can take it out when you have a quiet moment and use it to motivate you to complete any reaching out or loving intentions you wrote.

Finally, after the event, you can use it to reinforce the feelings of love that inevitably resulted from changing your patterned interactions with the various individuals you referred to.

33.
Applying the Principles and Practices to Weight Specifically

Getting Personal: The Steps I Took

I released approximately seventy pounds—I don't own a scale, so it could have been more. I used the concept of a self-care practice to design a strategy for changing my relationship with food. The following items represent the various steps I took.

Reconnecting with the Body

Your body is perfect. It has responded appropriately to the input you have given it. Being overweight was simply its way of letting you know that your patterns were out of balance. You body brought you to the incredibly knowledge you have gained from doing this process. Now, commit to loving and caring for your body. Work with your body every day to recognize the imbalances in your life – remember it will always let you know – just stay connected to your body by having a dialogue.

Having a dialogue with your body—as you did earlier in the book—is an important part of releasing weight and staying healthy. I recommend that you connect with you body daily (if not several times a day – especially before meals). Also, try to do the exercise from earlier in the book at least once a week (spend twenty to thirty minutes using your hands to physically connect with your body and have a dialogue with your body—followed by writing in your journal) Share your experience with any partners you may have in the process.

Snacking as a Strategy

Part of your strategy should certainly be nutritious meals, with the appropriate amounts of proteins, fruits, vegetables, and whole grains. But your body will get hungry and need food between meals—so have a plan to snack "consciously."

Unconscious snacking often represents a pattern, but planning small snacks between meals is part of a successful strategy. Don't wait until you feel like you are starving to eat—it will make you more susceptible to binges and unconscious choices. Plan small healthy snacks that fit your lifestyle and take them with you during your day to keep your body well-fueled. Many doctors and nutritionists recommend eating small meals every two to three hours suggesting that it actually speeds up you metabolism and helps you release weight.

It's important not to beat yourself up when you "forget" to plan your meals and snacks—it is hard to make self-honoring choices. Use these opportunities to learn, grow, and recommit to your process. If you notice emotional triggers sparking cravings for certain types of food, recognize the "win" in expanding your consciousness—you now have a choice as to how you want to address the discomfort.

No matter what happens, accept that you're doing the best you can. It's more important to practice compassion and self-forgiveness than to "get this right."

Write about your observations in your journal, and share them with any partners you may have in the process.

Activating Your Observer around "Tricky" Food Environments

At the market and at restaurants, it is especially important to activate your observer and make conscious choices. These are often the best places for you to work your process—learning and growing from the challenges you face.

Before you head to the market or go out to dinner, a good strategy for success is to eat a healthy snack so that you are not motivated by hunger—we tend to make impulsive choices when we are hungry.

At a restaurant, observe your reaction to the menu. Do you respond to visual stimuli, or do certain entrees or combinations trigger emotions? How does the excitement of being "out to dinner" trigger certain behaviors?

Consider under-ordering or splitting items with a companion—eating slowly and consciously. You can always order more.

Again, concentrate on how you feel inside. When you contemplate dessert or walk by the display cabinet or ice-cream station, do you experience anticipatory guilt? Is there a crisis of will, or are you able to *release* emotions and get past the moment of indecision?

Use your journal to be in relationship with yourself—try writing in your journal before you go and when you come back. Tracking your experience is an important part of releasing weight. Share your experience with any partners you may have in the process.

Affirmations and Intentions for Meals

Have affirmations and intentions that are specially designed for meals and snacks. Either out loud or in your head, use the "tools" to direct your experience.

Here are some examples (feel free to make up your own as well):

- I celebrate my ability to make healthy and wise decisions as I nourish my body.
- I recognize that my new inner authority is growing every day as I relate to food consciously. I choose to eat what my body needs.
- I am healthy, I love my body, and I offer it fuel and sustenance.
- Before partaking of this meal, I release any self-judgment, and any negativity. My intention is to joyfully nourish my body.

Note: You may find the tradition of saying "grace" to be a nice way to incorporate this affirmation and intention strategy. Just adjust the intention to fit the framework of your particular religious or spiritual tradition.

Write about your observations in your journal, and share them with any partners you may have in the process.

Rewards

For many of us who have struggled with weight, food has a distinct position in our psyche as a reward. Perhaps when we were kids, our parents took us out for ice cream if we got a good grade. Maybe special time alone with one of our parents meant getting candy or treats. It is very likely that major holidays focused on sweets.

As a parent, I can attest to how hard it is not to use food as a reward. It is even harder to refocus holidays and birthdays away from candy and dessert. Because my wife and I recognize the negative pattern that forms around this type of conditioning, we are very careful to give our children other things to look forward to.

The trick for us adults, who unconsciously associate food with reward, is to find ways of rewarding ourselves that don't involve food—specifically junk food. This takes some conscious reprogramming, but it can be done. I have found some excellent healthy alternatives that I have consciously relegated to "special occasions".

> My imperfections and failures are as much a blessing from God as my successes and my talents and I lay them both at his feet.
> —Gandhi

34.
Attitude of Gratitude

Getting Personal: Growing Grateful

When I was a kid, my mother constantly told me to say *thank you*. I don't think my child mind really understood why it was important. It just seemed like a nuisance, really.

As I grew into a teenager, some part of me may have understood the concept a little bit better, but it wasn't something I did enthusiastically.

As a young adult, I started to understand that I was fortunate to have some of the things that I had. I recognized that others didn't necessarily have what they wanted and some didn't even have what they needed. I began to show my gratitude.

In my late twenties and early thirties, life threw me just enough curve balls to knock me off my comfortable pedestal. From the low points in my life, I began to recognize the gifts that came and count the blessings. My gratitude began to build.

Now, in my forties, with enough life behind me to understand the precious gifts I have been given, I have learned to cherish my life. I have grown to become grateful, even for things that might not appear to be blessings at first.

A Constructive Vantage Point

The old saying about seeing the glass half full versus seeing the glass half empty is a nice way of understanding a view of life based on gratitude and appreciation for what is, instead of dwelling on lack or what is not. Having an attitude of gratitude is about viewing life from an empowered perspective.

Even when perceived setbacks occur, having the ability to be grateful for whatever learning might come from the situation will undoubtedly make the circumstances easier to deal with.

This is about staying positive and expressing the belief that everything that happens in life has the potential for a positive outcome, even when the situation seems negative. Having this perspective is like getting on the other side of your life and pushing it forward toward success and fulfillment, rather than letting unanticipated circumstances drag you backward.

By getting on the other side, I simply mean being an ally to yourself and continually putting things in perspective.

This is not about avoiding conflict or being delusional. This is about facing things and knowing that you will get through whatever the circumstances may be much more gracefully if you can view them from a constructive vantage point.

Positive Self-talk

There is a saying: "If you believe things will work out, you will see opportunities, while if you don't believe that things will work out, you will continually see obstacles and become frustrated." Use your affirmations to maintain a positive dialogue within your own mind.

Other people may react to your positive perspective—thinking you're crazy because you are focused on your progress and you're grateful for whatever comes up in life.

Attracting the Positive

Equally important, showing gratitude and remaining positive help build positive relationships, which in turn enhances your self-image.

Think about an experience where you met someone who immediately showed a negative side—they told you about their problems, complained about something, or were argumentative. Did you want to spend more time with this person? If you had to interact with a complainer, did you look forward to the prospect?

Think about a time when you unloaded on someone, gossiped or complained—how did you feel after the exchange? To the extent that you maintain an attitude of appreciation and gratitude, and sincerely try to see opportunities for growth instead of focusing on "problems," you will attract the same types of people into your life.

Healthy Boundaries

This is one of those areas where you may need to set boundaries. Decide (set an *intention*) that you will simply not participate in negativity so that a complainer will be forced to complain to someone else—to let his or her upset "land" elsewhere.

Maintaining your positive self-image may rely on deflecting negativity in your life. Try energetically (in your own mind) thanking a negative person for their input but choosing not to participate in their interpretation or negative perception. Be clear about what you let in.

As discussed earlier in this book, part of the process of releasing weight involves disconnecting from negative forces and directing your life toward positive possibilities by having a strategy for success.

You may choose to be grateful you have this personal process to help you make self honoring choices and direct your life toward fulfillment.

Exercise: Moving My Vision Forward with Gratitude

The premise of this exercise rests on the theory that you attract what you focus on. Gratitude is a major part of reframing your current circumstances and pointing your life in the direction you want to go, as opposed to focusing mainly on what you *don't want*. Often a minor adjustment in what we focus on can change the quality of our lives dramatically. Incremental minor adjustments can lead to monumental shifts in our experience.

Remember that you are the author of your own life, you are the authority on what you want, you know deep down what you are capable of, and you have all the tools necessary to attain the life you envision.

I would like you to revisit the life vision that you created earlier in this process (your life in five years). Adjust your vision by adding gratitude. This may be as simple as adding the phrase, "I am grateful for ..." prior to stating the identified experience you are going for.

35.
Creative Self-Expression

Getting Personal: My Need for Self-expression

I have found that I must express myself creatively in any and every way possible. Besides having been a professional actor, I paint, I write poetry, I sing, and I dance. Now, I am not necessarily sure whether or not I am particularly talented or skilled at any of the aforementioned forms of expression. I simply know that I am compelled to creatively express myself.

Here are three poems I wrote—I'm not sure if you will like them, but I do:

Natural Evolution, a.k.a. The Trials of Life

A moth is drawn to the flame that burns it.
There is a destiny in disaster that pulls us toward our greatness
by forcing us to face our fears.
Sometimes life requires us to find the bottom of the dark
shadow, lurking in our minds.
Somewhere in the deep we begin to lift.
When things have seemingly come apart completely, we
have the opportunity to step into a new becoming —wiser,
insightful, more reflective than before.
A breakthrough, born out of a breakdown, in the composure of
our lives.

Self-betrayal

Put on your faces.

Wear the mask of your own belonging.

The shelter from the storm of doubt and confusion.

Your mind's longing for safety and comfort.

You're free to hide.

Protection is an instinctual abandonment of truth.

Control, a repression of honesty and spontaneity.

Life cries out for you to surrender, to let it out.

But illusion clouds your perception and forces you further into self-deception.

The hole is so deep, the chasm so wide between authenticity and persona.

The prison doors shut a long time ago and you remain a captive in the hell of your own creation.

Let Love In

Intimacy takes bravery, the courage to risk inviting some deep longing into my life.

Hope, long since abandoned, emerges as I reach out for connection.

The promise of fulfillment, resurrected from a death brought about by disappointment and despair.

To believe again is perilous.

The broken trust of a painful past is swallowing my nerve.

There is no compromise, it's all or nothing.

It is just a moment, a flash decision

I cut it off

Maybe I'm just not ready.

Find Your Voice

This process is about meeting needs—as Maslow identified, there is a need for self-actualization. I don't necessarily believe that self-actualization is a destination; rather, I see it as a journey. Self-actualization, in my opinion, occurs when someone discovers a particular means of expression that "moves" them personally. Forgive the word "moves," but I don't have any other word to describe the experience. Each of us must find our own outlet—sometimes referred to as an artist's unique "voice." Creative self-expression is an opportunity to expand. Each one of us needs a way to grow beyond the limitations of our thoughts and ideas.

The process of unfolding, laid out in this book, would not be very valuable if it told you where you were going. There must be a process of discovery that is infinite and unique. It must be a process that can be explored time and time again in a multitude of different ways.

Exercise: Explore Your Creativity

This is the most open-ended of all my exercises—do whatever it is you want: paint, act, sing, dance, or write—or something else, I don't know. What I do know is that you must do it for yourself; don't be concerned with what others think. Give yourself permission to explore—and enjoy yourself. Then I want you to write in your journal about your experience.

What does this have to do with weight? You will release weight as you learn to love yourself; creative self-expression is an act of love.

36.
Where Do We Go from Here—Beyond Weight Release

Congratulations, you have learned a lot and come a long way. But you're probably wondering, "Now what?"

Point of Reference

If you have really "worked this process," chances are that you had a number of breakthrough moments. Breakthroughs can become important points of reference from which to establish a new, authentic sense of self.

I would guess, by now, you probably feel as though your life has already changed. For some of you, this change feels dramatic, while for others it may seem more subtle. Either way, you have taken significant steps toward *becoming the "you" you were born to be.* It is my sincere hope that the Service to Self™ process has provided you with tools that can continue to profoundly change your life.

Next Steps

The skills you have learned and the understanding you have gained are really a launching mechanism. It is the start of something wonderful, but the process is by no means complete. In fact, without a formal program to follow, you may fall back into old patterns of negative thinking and behavior.

Remember that there is a lot of support out there for the limitations you formerly bought into. The limitations, supported by media, culture, family, and religion, which you have worked so hard to overcome, are still present in your environment (unless you packed up and moved to where the Moken people live).

Sometimes completing a course of this kind can leave a person a bit lost when the program is finished, and the person unknowingly shifts back into old habits. I encourage you to stay connected through the "Wintention" link on the Service to Self™ Web site, where we are building a community to assist you in maintaining the progress you have made. This is a free and easy way to support yourself.

Stepping into the Mystery

Before you began this program, it is likely that the idea of "not knowing" scared you. Hopefully this process has given you tools and a new frame of reference to better embrace life as it comes.

With a strong sense of self, you can wake up to the adventure of life every morning with anticipation and excitement. Self-actualization is not an end but rather a means for embracing of a life journey, which is dynamic and ever-changing. Your potential for growth is limitless. Your evolution has no fixed conclusion.

If this attitude has become instilled in you, then I believe this book has really served its purpose. However, if your path still seems daunting, that is a strong indication that you have more work to do. Don't be discouraged if it feels as if you have a long way to go—there tend to be rather big leaps along the way. I often refer to this as a "click" (something clicks in your brain or understanding), which can happen at any time to bring about sudden clarity.

Embracing the Journey

The first step as you venture out with your new knowledge and skills is to find complementary books, audio CDs, groups, organizations, classes, and so on, to continue to expand your work on yourself. (Check the Resources section at the end of the book and go to the Service to Self™ Web site at www.servicetoself.com)

A commitment to learning and growing, when fully embraced, can give your life tremendous purpose. Your learning perspective toward life opens you up to new experiences as you begin to view things differently. Recognizing that each day you are alive is an opportunity to learn and grow makes every morning exciting. Things that before were judged as "bad" have now shifted to "interesting." Pain and discomfort can be viewed differently. Even death and tragedy can be seen in a new light.

> Finding meaning does not require us to live differently, it requires us to see our lives differently.
>
> —Rachel Naomi Remen

Remember to Sit in Your Discomfort

As I discussed earlier in the book, comfort food suggests the presence of discomfort. The goal is to embrace the discomfort and allow it to be your teacher and your guide. It will lead you to the unmet needs that are causing anxiety or distress.

Earlier in the process, when you learned how to acknowledge your needs and meet them in a new and healthy way, you were engaging in a sacred relationship. You developed a practice to support your needs, so that food no longer served to fill an emotional void. The relationship you fostered with your own discomfort is a tremendous gift. However, just like with other aspects of this process, the work is not over. The truth is that discomfort is part of life. However, I believe that what distinguishes extraordinary people from the ordinary is their ability to consciously choose their response to adversity and negativity.

I support you in your effort to continue to find ways to challenge yourself to meet discomfort head-on. If you have a fear of something, move through it by embracing it. Try to meet the fear directly and let it teach you about life and about yourself, you will be stronger for it. I know someone who was terrified of speaking in front of people; she joined Toastmasters to overcome her fear. Another woman I know was very afraid of heights, so she did a "ropes course," where she worked in a safe setting to release her fear. I personally take yoga to help me learn to be with my body and overcome the discomfort I feel physically.

Most people think that courage is the absence of fear. The absence of fear is not courage; the absence of fear is some kind of brain damage. Courage is the capacity to go ahead in spite of the fear, or in spite of the pain. When you do that, you will find that overcoming that fear will not only make you stronger but will be a big step forward toward maturity. —M. Scott Peck

Pain

I am not suggesting that you necessarily invite painful situations into your life. But I am clear that pain is part of life. The challenge is to deal effectively with pain, learn from it, and even be grateful for it. The experience of pain shifts dramatically when you have a "learning perspective toward life." Remember that you can reframe painful situations from a positive perspective.

Denying or medicating pain prolongs and exacerbates it. Only by embracing pain and allowing it to teach us can we overcome it. Our resistance—the sense that painful experiences shouldn't be happening—is the true cause of our suffering. When we embrace pain, suffering goes away and the situation is "just painful."

Avoiding Pitfalls—"Fixing" Others

It is very tempting when you have new knowledge that has served you well to want to share it with other people. And I encourage you to do that, but I suggest that you limit your discussions to your own experiences and how you have found the book and exercises helpful. I would love for you to recommend the book or introduce others to the Web site, but please resist the temptation to try to solve other people's problems with your new knowledge.

Just because you have new insights into the dynamics that promote healthy thinking and behavior in your life, it does not necessarily mean that you can or should fix other people. In fact, there is a strong likelihood that your good intentions will be misunderstood, seen as criticism, or taken as offensive. This may negatively impact your own hard work and positive results.

By now, you understand that the nature of the conditioned thinking and behavior that you have personally overcome is defensive. Thus, any attempt to "help" a defensive person will in all likelihood be viewed as an attack.

By reading and participating in the exercises in this book you have learned to accept yourself. You came to understand that the patterns of behavior you engaged in made sense. If you are around someone who is struggling with similar issues, try to accept them for where they are. Remember where you were emotionally, physically, psychologically, and spiritually when you picked up this book. Now imagine how you might have responded before you began this process, if someone had sprung these concepts on you. Chances are, you wouldn't have been able to recognize their value by having them thrust upon you before you were ready.

Allow People the Dignity of Their Own Process
I believe that each person is on his or her own unique journey. Remember the example of my daughter climbing on furniture and falling off; it is important to recognize that we all need to fall in our own way to learn to climb. Each person has his or her own process of learning. The inclination to want to save others is not necessarily rooted in what is in that person's highest good.

Trying to save people from themselves is not just futile, it is often counterproductive.

Let me be clear: If someone is going to get hit by a bus if they step off the curb, and you recognize that they don't see the bus coming, by all means warn them. This is not about wanting bad things to happen to other people. It is simply a matter of letting people figure things out in their own way and in their own time.

If you are in a position to be a teacher and the other person is willing to be your student, then teach them. However, if you are trying to teach someone who is not ready to learn, then you are doing no one any good.

If you want to teach, then be intentional and the universe will provide you a receptive student. It may not be the person or group you expected, or the situation you might have chosen, but I believe that if you are really ready to teach, then students and opportunities will start showing up in your life. Still, it is hard not to want to help the people we love.

So How Do We Help Our Loved Ones?

I have three children; as a parent, I have an inherent desire to try to save them from heartache, loss, and disappointment. But children are pretty adamant on learning their own lessons. We can tell them a thousand times not to do something, but often they will do it anyway—they are just learning.

Don't get me wrong; I talk to my children. Besides encouraging them (which I see as my primary job), I instruct them and occasionally discipline them. But the words I speak often fall on deaf ears. Often the same advice I give (which they ignored) can be viewed as the wisdom of a sage when it comes from someone else. Children inherently have a difficult time accepting what their parents tell them.

Besides being a parent, I am also the child of two very loving and well-meaning parents. I have a hard time hearing their advice; although I confess that as I have gotten older, I am more and more appreciative of their wisdom. But in general, I still often perceive their counsel as criticism (which I know is not how it is intended).

Model Change

The main opportunity I have to teach anyone is by example. When I model behavior, people pay attention, whether consciously or unconsciously. My suggestion to you is to do the same. Let your change be the lesson. If you stand in the integrity of who you have evolved into, friends and family members will eventually take notice. As you make self-honoring choices and release weight people will surely ask you how you did it. The simple truth is that you learned to love yourself. However, this explanation may illicit more confusion than clarity. Don't try to explain if they are not ready to hear.

If you continue to grow in your own quality of life and purpose, then ultimately loved ones will open up to the approach you have taken.

Respect Their Process and Remember Your First Steps

A child falls down countless times when learning to walk. As a parent, mainly you just watched. Perhaps you put out a finger as a guide, or maybe you moved a piece of furniture so that the child wouldn't bump her head. Well, that is the same way you should introduce the concepts you have learned to a friend or family member. Give it to them in small, bite-sized pieces, checking to make sure they have digested each piece before the next serving. Some of your best action may involve "not doing". Just have a loving, open heart and energetically extend that love out to them.

My Process

I developed the Service to Self™ process from different programs, books, and traditions for one reason—to assist me. I have refined it, and I practice it for one reason—to assist me. The Service to Self™ process is not just a theory; it is my personal process that I work with every day in my own life. The impact it has had on me is what compelled me to write this book. I offer it to you, in service to your growth.

Over the years, I have come to recognize that the fundamental component of my personal process involves checking in regularly. Sometimes my conscious observer kicks in as I experience some energetic shift in my body. Other times, the outer world reminds me to check in because circumstances around me start getting a little tense (or intense). If I get disconnected from myself, go unconscious, and stop paying attention, I find myself sick or injured. The universe tends to wake me up.

Part of my relationship with myself is honoring my needs. As much as possible, I get my needs met consciously by making self-honoring choices. If I find myself making unconscious choices, then my true needs are very rarely met.

Being intentional is critical to my happiness and well-being. If I am not living my life in alignment with my intention and vision, then there are negative consequences. I am the author of my own story and I choose to write a tale of fulfillment, gratitude, and service.

To My Reader

My intention in writing this book was to offer you the gift of my own learning, in service to you becoming the "you" you were born to be. Embracing your life experience and sharing your gifts, talents, and abilities as a unique individual—"the authentic you"—is what the world vitally needs.

Good luck and God bless you.

Appendix

Resources

A New Earth: Awakening to Your Life's Purpose, by Eckhart Tolle, Penguin; Reprint edition (2008) (Oprah's Book Club, Selection 61).

Anatomy of the Spirit: The Seven Stages of Power and Healing, by Caroline Myss, Three Rivers Press; First edition (1997).

Emotional Awareness: Overcoming the Obstacles to Psychological Balance and Compassion, by the Dalai Lama and Paul Ekman, Times Books (2008).

Food and Emotions, by Mary Turck, Capstone Press (2001).

Foundation for Human Enrichment, by Dr. Peter M. Levine. *http://www.traumahealing.com/*

Healing and the Mind, by Bill Moyers, Main Street Books (1995).

Molecules of Emotion, by Candace Pert, Scribner (1997).

Nonviolent Communication: A Language of Compassion, by Marshall B. Rosenberg, Puddledancer Press (2003).

Riding the Dragon: The Power of Committed Relationship, by Rhea Powers and Gawain Bantle, North Star Publications (1995).

The Art of Happiness: A Handbook for Living, by the Dalai Lama and Howard C. Cutler, Riverhead Hardcover (1998).

The Biology of Belief: Unleashing the Power of Consciousness, Matter, & Miracles, by Bruce H. Lipton, Hay House (2008).

The Four Agreements, by Don Miguel Ruiz, Available on CD: 152 minutes (Unabridged), Amber-Allen Audio Publishing (2003).

The Intention Experiment: Using Your Thoughts to Change Your Life and the World, by Lynne McTaggart, Free Press (2008).

The Journey to Greatness: And How to Get There! by Noah benShea, Corwin Press (2005).

The Tibetan Book of Living and Dying, by Sogyal Rinpoche, Harper San Francisco (1992).

Toward a Psychology of Being, 3rd Edition, by Abraham H. Maslow, Wiley (1998).

Unstuck: Your Guide to the Seven-Stage Journey Out of Depression, by James S. Gordon, MD, Penguin Press HC, (2008).

Wherever You Go, There You Are: Mindfulness Meditation in Everyday Life, by Jon Kabat-Zinn, Hyperion (1994).

What We May Be, by Piero Ferrucci, Jeremy P. Tarcher, Inc. (2004).

Women Who Run with the Wolves, by Clarissa Pinkola Estes, Ballantine Books (1996).

Twelve Keys to Personal Fulfillment

These twelve words find their way into every level of the process I teach. We, at Service to Self™, believe that they represent principles that lead to happiness and contentment.

1. **Accept** that everything is perfect. When viewed accurately, your life is a synchronistic series of events. You have been on a magnificent journey to get to this moment.

2. **Acknowledge** yourself for the choices you have made. You have faced a lot, and you have done well. The very fact that you are reading this suggests that you are courageous.

3. **Recognize** the genius in the skills, talents, and gifts you have.

4. **Track** your experience and develop an observer—watch your negative self-talk.

5. **Identify** misinterpretations based on shame, blame, and guilt.

6. **Release** judgment as you learn to view your experience and the experience of others from a higher (and more accurate) perspective.

7. **Reframe** your experience from a place of compassion and look for the learning opportunities in what you may have previously regarded as negative.

8. **Surrender** your life to your higher purpose (or God, if that language suits you). You are on a special path intended to uplift you and those around you.

9. **Support** yourself by surrounding yourself with allies. Practice positive self-talk. Remember that being effective involves finding support for things you are not naturally good at or need help with.

10. **Celebrate** accomplishments—yours and others'. Always maintain an "attitude of gratitude" for the blessings in your life.

11. **Course Correct**—gently recognize when you are on a course that will produce an outcome you don't necessarily want, and gracefully adjust the course you are on.

12. **Teach** others to accept and love themselves by modeling confidence, peacefulness, and contentment.

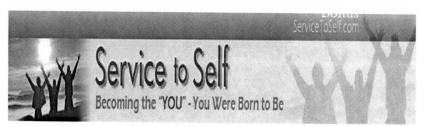

We are committed to your succcess

Your Free Bonus
Our way of saying "Thank You" for buying this book

Visit
www.servicetoself.com/anewyou

The greatest testament to the quality of our products is your success. No two people have the same needs. The link provided offers valuable tools that can be applied immediately to achieve LASTING Weight Release.

www.servicetoself.com

BUY A SHARE OF THE FUTURE IN YOUR COMMUNITY

These certificates make great holiday, graduation and birthday gifts that can be personalized with the recipient's name. The cost of one S.H.A.R.E. or one square foot is $54.17. The personalized certificate is suitable for framing and will state the number of shares purchased and the amount of each share, as well as the recipient's name. The home that you participate in "building" will last for many years and will continue to grow in value.

Here is a sample SHARE certificate:

YES, I WOULD LIKE TO HELP!

*I support the work that Habitat for Humanity does and I want to be part of the excitement! As a donor, I will receive periodic updates on your construction activities but, more importantly, I know my gift will help a family in our community realize the dream of homeownership. **I would like to SHARE in your efforts against substandard housing in my community!** (Please print below)*

PLEASE SEND ME _____ SHARES at $54.17 EACH = $ $_____

In Honor Of: _____

Occasion: (Circle One)   HOLIDAY   BIRTHDAY   ANNIVERSARY

      OTHER: _____

Address of Recipient: _____

Gift From: _____ *Donor Address:* _____

Donor Email: _____

I AM ENCLOSING A CHECK FOR $ $_____ PAYABLE TO HABITAT FOR HUMANITY <u>OR</u> PLEASE CHARGE MY VISA OR MASTERCARD *(CIRCLE ONE)*

Card Number _____ Expiration Date: _____

Name as it appears on Credit Card _____ Charge Amount $ _____

Signature _____

Billing Address _____

Telephone # Day _____ Eve _____

PLEASE NOTE: Your contribution is tax-deductible to the fullest extent allowed by law.
Habitat for Humanity • P.O. Box 1443 • Newport News, VA 23601 • 757-596-5553
www.HelpHabitatforHumanity.org